SEANNA MILLER

D0559858

THE
HAYSTACK
SYNDROME

Other North River Press Books by
Eliyahu M. Goldratt

The Goal
The Race (with Robert E. Fox)
Theory of Constraints
It's Not Luck
Critical Chain

THE HAYSTACK SYNDROME

Sifting Information Out
of
The Data Ocean

Eliyahu M. Goldratt

North River Press

Additional copies of this book can be obtained from your local bookstore or the publisher:

The North River Press
Publishing Corporation
P.O. Box 567
Great Barrington, MA 01230
(800) 486-2665 or (413) 528-0034

www.northriverpress.com

Copyright © 1990 Dr. Eliyahu M. Goldratt

All rights reserved. No part of this work may be reproduced or utilized in any form or by any means, electronic or mechanical, including photocopying, recording, or any information storage and retrieval system, without permission in writing from the publisher.

Manufactured in the United States of America

ISBN: 0-88427-089-0

Table of Contents

v

THE
HAYSTACK
SYNDROME

PART ONE

FORMALIZING THE DECISION PROCESS

1. *Data, information and the decision process—how they relate*

We are drowned in oceans of data; nevertheless it seems as if we seldom have sufficient information.

Do you agree? Does it bother you?

If so, why don't we discuss it—not just idle discussion, crying on each other's shoulders, finding comfort in telling war stories. Let's discuss it more seriously, almost as if we pretend that "you and I can change the world." Let's actually attempt to find a practical solution to this horrendous problem, one that can really work.

Where should we start?

The obvious logical place would be to define precisely what we mean by the words *data* and *information*. What is the real distinction between them? This is the core of our complaint, isn't it? Are these words already defined? Maybe they are in dictionaries and some textbooks, but certainly not in practice.

How many times have you seen a computer package offered under the title of "information system" that, after a casual examination, you immediately discovered was just a "data system"?!

What is data?

An address of a supplier is data. A purchase price of an item is data. Each detail of a product's design or the contents of a

3

warehouse is also data. It seems as if every string of characters that describes something, anything, about our reality, is data. If this is the case, what is left to be called information?

It looks as if the only way to answer this question is by refuting what we just postulated. The address of a supplier is data, but for the person who has to send a complaint letter, this address is definitely information. You might call the content of a warehouse data, but if you are looking to find whether or not an urgent client order can be immediately fulfilled, then it is information. The same string of characters that we refer to as data, might be called, under some circumstances, information. It appears that information is in the eyes of the beholder.

Are we going in circles? Not necessarily so. Intuitively we understand information to be that portion of the data which impacts our actions, or if missing or not available will impact our actions. For different people or even for the same person at different times, the same string of characters might be data or information.

We almost cannot escape the realization that the distinction between data and information does not lie in the content of a given string of characters. It lies more in its relationship to the required decision. If we don't know in advance what type of decision we are going to make, if we don't know in advance what exactly we will need, then every piece of data might at some time be considered information. Is it any wonder it is so difficult to distinguish a data bank from an information system?

Can we, in our changing world, ever be in a position where we can distinguish, a priori, what is information? Is it at all possible to design something that we can wholeheartedly call an information system, especially when that system is not intended to be used for just one type of decision, for just one management function?

We would like to have a system that will supply information to all the managers in an organization, for all types of decisions. From what we've said so far, it looks as if, at any given point in time, most of the content of such a system will actually be just data. So what?! If it will supply the information, does it really matter?!

This is exactly the line of reasoning that has led us into the current systems. You see, the next natural step will be to start asking ourselves what type of possible questions we might face in the future. Not just we, but every function in the organization. Then, we happily jump into the next step—trying to define which pieces of data/information will be required. From there it is just a small step until we're totally immersed in the effort of defining the appropriate input formats, file layouts, query procedures, etc. . . . The road to the mammoth task of collecting and maintaining oceans of data is now wide open. The same trend also impacts the format of the output reports. They will be voluminous, trying to cover every possible question. Yes, in the last few years personal computers and online query capabilities have, to some extent, eliminated this phenomenon, but not the underlying thinking that led to it.

In Israel, there is a legend that I cannot testify is true, but I would not be surprised if such a case really happened. Ten years ago, the only practical way to retrieve information from the computer was by printed reports. At that time, the central computer department of the Israeli army was considering the then new technology of the mammoth laser printer as an answer to their prayers. A captain in that department, probably very arrogant and also a little bit irresponsible, decided to address the same problem in quite an original way. Without any approval, he gave an instruction to stop printing, dispatching, and sending any report that contained more than 100 pages. At that time, when computer decentralization was just a thought, numerous copies of these reports were spread from the central site to numerous points in the army. The legend recounts that only one single complaint arrived from the receiving points. The person who complained was a guy whose job it was to neatly file the reports.

Every manager in a large organization can very easily relate to this legend. If this particular story is a legend, many, many similar stories are definitely reality. Besides, what was our original complaint? We are drowning in oceans of data. The situation today is so bad that in public appearances, whenever I raise the suggestion of connecting the printers directly to the shredders, the audience responds with laughter and cheers. Somewhere along the line we have taken a wrong turn. Somewhere along the line there must be a logical flaw. Information systems may not preclude the necessity for data banks, but certainly information systems must be totally different entities. If they are to be effective, they cannot be identical to our current data banks.

Let's go back to the point where the distinction between data and information was stated. We have attempted to define information as the data required to reach the decision. This attempt didn't carry us too far, but nevertheless, intuitively we feel that information can be defined only within the framework of how we make decisions. Maybe we should define information not as "the data required to answer a question" but as "the answer to the question asked."

This is not just a semantic difference. View it for a minute or two, and you too will probably feel as uneasy as I do. You see, the minute that we define information as the answer to the question asked, it means that information is not input to the decision process, it is the output of the decision process. Accepting this definition implies that the decision process itself must be imbedded in an information system. This will require the frightening task of achieving a very precise formalization of the decision process. In our case it definitely means to open a new Pandora's Box—in industry today the decision process itself is changing.

The eighties are viewed, by more and more professionals, as the decade in which a second industrial revolution occurred—a revolution in the way that we regard the essence of managing our business, a revolution that impacts the basic procedures by which managers make decisions. Any logical discussion of the composition and structure of information systems must be done within the framework of the decision process. Thus, we cannot escape from the necessity of analyzing the new management philosophy that has started to emerge.

At first sight, it might look like a huge deviation. We would like our discussion to lead to information systems, and suddenly we may have to spend considerable time analyzing management philosophies? But it is unavoidable as long as we want to explore the possibility of finding a robust method that will lead to the creation of satisfactory information systems. Besides, maybe the simplicity that characterizes these new movements will lead to new, much simpler, and more powerful solutions for our subject as well.

2. *What a company tries to achieve*

"Quality is Job One." "Inventory is a liability." "Balance flow, not capacity." Those are just a few of the slogans that have shaken the foundation of industrial management. In the eighties, we witnessed three powerful movements—Total Quality Management (TQM), Just In Time (JIT), and Theory of Constraints (TOC)—that challenged almost everything that was previously accepted. Those movements each had their modest start in some local technique. But all have evolved with breathtaking speed.

We are beginning to realize that our initial perception of what these movements encompassed is much too narrow. I think that you will probably agree with me when I describe the change in perception in the following way:

IT IS ABOUT TIME TO REALIZE THAT JIT'S PRIMARY FOCUS IS NOT THE REDUCTION OF INVENTORY ON THE SHOP FLOOR. IT IS NOT JUST A MECHANICAL KANBAN TECHNIQUE. IT IS DEFINITELY A NEW OVERALL MANAGEMENT PHILOSOPHY.

IT IS ABOUT TIME TO REALIZE THAT TOC'S PRIMARY FOCUS IS NOT BOTTLENECKS ON THE SHOP FLOOR. IT IS NOT JUST A MECHANICAL OPTIMIZED PRODUCTION TECHNIQUE. IT IS

DEFINITELY A NEW OVERALL MANAGEMENT PHILOSOPHY.

IT IS ABOUT TIME TO REALIZE THAT TQM'S PRIMARY FOCUS IS NOT THE QUALITY OF THE PRODUCTS. IT IS NOT JUST A MECHANICAL STATISTICAL PROCESS CONTROL TECHNIQUE. IT IS DEFINITELY A NEW OVERALL MANAGEMENT PHILOSOPHY.

I don't have to ask if you have noticed the similarities. But rather than feeling good about our new understanding, I think we should ask ourselves the two unavoidable emerging questions.

1. What is really "new" in these new overall management philosophies? As long as these movements were understood to be local techniques, we understood and appreciated quite well what is new in them. But now our intuitive understanding is accepting a very demanding phrase— NEW OVERALL MANAGEMENT PHILOSOPHY. This is a little bit hard to swallow. The new local techniques certainly do not justify these high words. First of all, these movements are mainly restricted to the production arena. So why the usage of the word "overall" ? Second, as powerful as they are, they still do not deserve to be called management philosophies. A much better verbalization of what these movements have brought with them is needed to justify our intuitive understanding.
2. How many new management philosophies are there—one or three? Once we verbalize our current understanding and express it precisely in words, then, and only then, will we be in a position to see whether or not we are facing a choice.

As long as we avoid answering the two questions set forth above, we will find ourselves in the current situation, where we have added on top of the "End of the Month Syndrome" what can only be described as the "Beginning of the Month Improvement Project." The place to start to search for an answer to these questions is obvious. A phrase like NEW OVERALL MANAGEMENT PHILOSOPHY can be justified only by a major change in the foundation. Any improvement, no matter how big, in a relatively minor subject, will never justify such a demanding title.

Probably the most fundamental question we can ask is "Why is an organization built?" to start with. I don't believe that any organization has been built merely for its own existence. Every organization was built to achieve a purpose. Thus, whenever we debate any action in any section of any organization, the only way to hold a logical discussion is by judging the impact of the action on the overall purpose of the organization.

Quite trivial. But out of this short argument, the foundation of any organization is revealed. The first thing that must be clearly defined is the overall purpose of the organization—or as I prefer to call it, the organization's goal. The second thing is measurements. Not just any measurements, but measurements that will enable us to judge the impact of a local decision on the global goal.

If we want to look for something significant, the first place to look is at the goal of the organization, and then, if we haven't found any change there, at its measurements.

Let's start with the organization's goal. You have probably found, as I have, that in some cases it is quite hard to get a precise determination. So let's spend some time in clarifying this issue to ourselves. Who has the right to determine the organization's goal? It doesn't take a phenomenal brain to reach the obvious answer. The goal of the organization must be determined solely by the owners of that organization. Any other answer will force us to redefine the meaning of the word "ownership."

Here we face a problem. We are experienced enough to know that no matter which organization we are dealing with, almost all of them face some power groups. A power group is a group that has the power to ruin, or at least severely damage, the organization, if the group dislikes some aspects of the organization's behavior. It looks as if we have to give those power groups a say. But giving them a say will immediately mean that the owners do not have the SOLE right to determine the goal. A catch-22.

The way out of this dichotomy is to distinguish clearly between the goal of an organization and necessary conditions imposed on its behavior. The organization should strive to meet its goal within the boundaries imposed by the power groups, striving to fulfill its purpose without violating any of the externally imposed necessary conditions.

For an industrial enterprise, clients are definitely a power group. They do impose necessary conditions, like a minimum level of customer service and a minimum level of product quality. If these minimum conditions are not met, the clients will simply stop purchasing from the organization, and it will face extinction. But certainly no one will suggest that our clients have the right to dictate or even interfere in what should be our organization's goal.

The organization's employees are a power group. They impose necessary conditions, like minimum job security and minimum wages. If the organization violates these necessary conditions, it faces the risk of a strike. But this does not mean that the employees—as employees—have the right to determine the organization's goal.

Our government is a power group. Governments, even local ones, impose necessary conditions, like maximum levels of air or water pollution. If a plant violates these necessary conditions, it faces the very real threat of being closed down, regardless of how profitable it is. But that does not mean that our government has the right to tell us what should be our organization's goal—as long as we are not in Russia. Over there it is perfectly right, because under the communist system, the government IS the owner of the organizations.

The goal of a company is solely in the hands of it owners. If we are dealing with an industrial enterprise, we call the owners of the enterprise "shareholders." So the question "What is the goal of the enterprise?" is exactly equivalent to the question "Why did the shareholders invest their money in the enterprise?" In order to achieve what?

In light of the above, what do you think of a company that states "Our goal is to provide the best quality products coupled with the best customer service?" Such a company probably has very unique shareholders. Its shareholders have apparently invested their money in the company so that they can brag at a cocktail party that their company provides the best customer service. Is it your company? Most probably not.

Or consider a company that states that its goal is to become number one; they are going to capture the largest market share. The shareholders probably invested their money in that company because they are power maniacs. But the most ridiculous statement, which unfortunately can be found in so many textbooks, is the statement that the company's goal is to survive. Such a statement definitely places most shareholders in the category of altruistic human beings.

If a company has even one share traded on Wall Street, the goal has been loudly and clearly stated. We invest our money, through Wall Street, in order to make more money now as well as in the future. That's the goal of any company whose shares are traded in the open market.

It should be noted that the generic statement is not "A company's goal is to make more money now as well as in the future." The generic statement is "The owners have the sole right to determine the goal." If we are dealing with a privately held company, no outsider can predict its goal. We must directly ask the owners.

It is quite disturbing to see so many publicly held companies where top management confuses the necessary conditions, the means, and the goal. Such confusion so often leads to misdirection and long-term destruction of the company. Customer service, product quality, good human relationships, are definitely necessary conditions, sometimes even means. But they are not the goal. The employees of a company should serve the shareholders—that's what they are getting paid for. Serving clients is just a means to the real task, serving the company's shareholders.

Nothing new here. Yes, sometimes a lot of confusion, but nothing new. So in order to find out what is new in those overall management philosophies, we don't have any choice but to apply our analysis and examination to the second fundamental entity—the measurements.

3. *Getting a hold on measurements*

Measurements are a direct result of the chosen goal. There is no way that we can select a set of measurements before the goal is defined. For example, to use money-based measurements to judge the performance of an army or a church is quite ridiculous.

In this text we will engage ourselves in the broad, but still not generic, case of a company whose goal is to make more money now as well as in the future. Thus, for other types of companies, the following analysis does not apply, even though I believe the logical process is probably the same.

We judge the performance of a company by its financial statements. When we say "bottom line" we're not referring just to one number, but two. The first one is an absolute measurement, like Net Profit. We report this number on the profit and loss (P&L) statement. The second is a relative measure and thus a pure number, like Return on Investment, return on total assets, or return on shareholders' equity. The second measurement is reported today on the balance sheet. There is a third financial statement which does not represent a measurement, but rather a very important necessary condition—the cash statement.

It is very important to note that these bottom line measurements are not the measurements that we are after. These measurements are capable of measuring the goal. However, the measurements which we refer to as the fundamental quantities are the measurements that enable us to judge the impact of a local decision on the company's goal. Every manager knows all too well that the bottom line measurements are quite impotent in judging the impact of a local decision.

What are the measurements that we use to judge local decisions? No, we are certainly not going to immerse ourselves in the endless task of listing all the local measurements used by the various departments of various companies. This is a fruitless job, especially when we remember that in many places, it seems as if the dominant measurements are strongly dependent on the current mood of the top guy, the day of the week, and possibly the weather as well. Rather, it's much simpler, and certainly more fruitful, to engage ourselves in some mental exercises.

Such mental exercises are one of the most powerful tools used in physics. They are called *Gedunken* experiments. They are experiments that are never done in reality, you just think about them (*Gedunken* means "thinking" in German). Your experience is broad enough to indicate the results exactly, so there is no need to actually carry them out. Let's do such a *Gedunken* experiment.

First, we should describe the company. We are interested in finding measurements for a company whose goal is to make more money now as well as in the future. What does this company generate? Basic metals? Sophisticated electronic equipment? Commodities? Does it really matter? Yes. What we must realize is that all the examples discussed above describe the physical products of the company, not what it generates. As long as we define its goal the way we have, what the company generates (or should generate) is definitely only one thing—money. Thus, we can safely describe the company as "a money-making machine."

We have already agreed on the goal—we have already decided that we would like to have a money-making machine. Imagine that you just entered the only shop that sells money-making machines. There are many money-making machines in this shop, and you definitely want to choose one of them. What input do you need from the salesman in order to make your choice? Once we verbalize what input we need, we have actually verbalized measurements.

But in addition to the measurements, we might also verbalize some necessary conditions. Since this experiment is to find the measurements, and since necessary conditions might drastically differ from one company to another, let's assume that all the machines in the shop meet all our necessary conditions. Thus, if we can clearly verbalize what we need to know to make the choice, we are actually verbalizing the needed measurements. Remember, we can expect the salesman to supply us with data about each machine; we should not expect, or even desire, that this person will make the choice for us.

The first needed piece of information that jumps into our mind is, "How much money does the machine make?" But let's be careful. Suppose that the salesman will tell us, "This first machine makes one million dollars—this other machine, only half a million." Suppose that we have chosen the first machine, just to find that it does generate one million dollars, but in ten years. The other machine generates half a million in just one year. Do you think that we will hold a grudge against the salesman? Why? He answered exactly what we asked. The problem is not with the salesman, it's with us. We haven't asked what we intended to.

What do we really want to know? The rate. So let's ask it. "What is the rate at which the machine generates money?" Let's remember that the machine we refer to here is not a physical machine. It is our entire company, and the rate at which the money is generated takes into account our entire company, after it interacts with its surroundings.

Let's examine the question once again. What is the rate at which the machine generates money? Suppose that the salesman tells us that one particular machine generates money at the rate of one million dollars per month, and another at just half a million per month. We choose the first one, just to find that three months later it totally disintegrates, while the other ma-

chine goes for ever. Do you think that we will like the salesman?

Once again, we must clarify what we really meant by our
question. We certainly did not intend to ask for just the current
rate of generating money. We have asked for the rate as a function of time. If we would have made ourselves clearly understood, the salesman would have been forced to tell us that the
rate of the first machine drops to zero after three months. Why
should we waste time blaming others, when we can prevent
such problems simply by expressing ourselves more clearly?

There is another issue that we must clarify. We would like to
know the probability of the salesman's predictions coming true.
Every numerical answer is just a guesstimate. We should demand to know the reliability of his predictions. In this light, we
have to understand our question—what is the rate at which the
"machine" generates money?

Is this enough? Definitely not. The cost of the machine is
certainly on our minds. But let's be careful for a change. What
do we mean by "cost?" Cost is one of those very dangerous
words that has more than one interpretation. We may ask,
"What is the cost of the machine?" and mean the purchase
price. But we may ask the same question and mean the operating expense—how much it costs to operate it. One interpretation is in the realm of investments, the other in the realm of
spending. These are quite different interpretations. Let's remember we might become very rich by prudent investments,
but certainly not by spending our money. However, both interpretations are of vital importance.

How should we phrase our questions? To ask the purchase
price of the machine is not enough. We might face some unpleasant surprises when we find that the physical dimensions
will force us to move a building, or that the amount of inventory that the machine has to carry in its belly is even more
expensive than the price of the machine itself. I would suggest
that we ask, "How much money is captured by the machine?"
And once again, let's insist on having the answer as a function
of time and with the appropriate probabilities.

Money captured by the machine does not mean that we do not own this money. It only means that the minute that we remove even part of this money, the machine is then incapable of continuing to produce, or at least its performance will be degraded. This is quite different from the following question that we still have to ask. "How much money will we have to pour into the machine on an ongoing basis to turn the machine's wheels?"

4. *Defining Throughput*

Three simple questions: How much money is generated by our company? How much money is captured by our company? And how much money do we have to spend to operate it? The measurements are intuitively obvious. What is needed is to turn these questions into formal definitions. These formal definitions I have already proposed in *The Goal.*

The first one is THROUGHPUT. Throughput is defined as: The rate at which the system generates money through sales.

As a matter of fact, we will get a more precise definition if we will erase the last two words—through sales. You see, if the system generates money by earning interest at a bank, it is definitely throughput. Why did I add these two words? Because of a common behavior in our companies. Most production managers think that if they have produced something, it deserves to be called throughput. What is your opinion? If we have produced something, but have not yet sold it, can we really call it throughput?

This distortion is not just confined to production. How does the financial group react if you double your finished goods inventory? If the products are not obsolete, what will be the financial judgment of this action? The controller will tell you that, according to the way that he is supposed to treat the numbers, you have done a very good thing. You have absorbed more overhead and the financial statement will show an increase in

19

net profit. Our business intuition certainly does not support this. Throughput cannot possibly be associated with shuffling money internally. Throughput means to bring fresh money from the outside, thus the additional words—through sales.

It should be emphasized that throughput should not be confused with sales. Throughput is the rate at which the system generates money through sales. What is the difference? Suppose that we sold a product for $100. This does not yet mean that throughput increased by $100. It might be that in the product sold, there are materials and parts that we purchased from our vendors for, let's say, $30. The $30 is not money generated by our system, it is money generated by our vendor's system. It is just money flowing through our system. Thus, in this case, the throughput will be increased by only $70. Throughput is the selling price minus the amounts we paid to our vendors for the items that went into the product sold, no matter when we actually bought these items.

In addition to purchased parts and materials, there are other amounts we have to subtract from the selling price in order to compute throughput, We have to deduct subcontracting, commission paid to an external salesman, customs duties, and even transportation, if we do not own the transportation channel. All those amounts are not money generated by our system.

You might have noticed that the throughput definition requires that we determine the point in time when a sale occurred. Today, two conventions are widely used. One is when the money actually changes hands. The other, more popular, way, is the accrual technique, which is supposed to be when the transaction is irreversible. Unfortunately, this practice is not strictly obeyed in many companies.

In many consumer-goods industries, the products are not sold directly to the consumer by the manufacturer, but rather through distribution chains. In most cases, those distribution channels reserve the right to return merchandise without even an explanation. It seems very inappropriate that a sale is recorded when products are shipped to the distribution companies, even though the transaction is certainly reversible.

Can you believe that some companies refund the distributor according to the current price, not the price paid? You are probably aware that in the consumer-goods industry "promotions," or as consumers call it, "sales," is the name of the game. Which means it is possible for the distributor to buy merchandise during the promotion period, wait two months, return it, and make 20 percent in two months. This is even better than the Mafia's business. Does it really happen? On a much larger scale than any outsider would imagine. I asked the president of such a consumer-products company why his company, after being in business for fifty years, did not block this loophole. His answer was: "You are wrong, we have not been in business for fifty years. We have been in business for 200 quarters." The sale is reported this quarter, the return will be in the next quarter.

This phenomenon is not exactly funny, but it certainly highlights the fact that the point of sale should not be the time that money changes hands. Unfortunately, negligence in determining the point of sale has even more far-reaching ramifications.

We are all aware that the dealers of most American and European car companies hold about a 90-day supply of cars. These cars have been reported as sales by the car companies. The dealers have actually purchased them. But just peer into the details a little bit more, and you will be amazed. It turns out that, in most cases, the dealer has purchased the car by borrowing the money from the car company. What is the car company's collateral? Just the car itself. If the dealer is stuck with a large stock when the model year changes, who do you think gives the rebates? Not the dealer.

For all practical purposes, for all sound business purposes, despite the cars being in the dealers' hands, they should not have been declared as sales by the car companies. This method leads to a devastating conflict between short term—sales this quarter—and long term—responding quickly to the market and thus increasing future sales. This problem is not just confined to the car companies, it is the problem of every company that sells through a distribution system rather than directly to the end consumer. It is important here to distinguish between a customer and a consumer. The sale should be recorded when an irrevocable transaction has occured with the consumer, and not just with the customer. Excess products in the distribution pipes just increase the distance between the producer and its ultimate client. This is almost a recipe for a future loss in throughput. To remove this conflict between short and long term, we can simply redefine the point of sale.

5. *Removing the overlap between Inventory and Operating Expense*

The second measurement is inventory. Inventory is defined as all the money the system invests in purchasing things the system intends to sell. Why the words "all the money?" Somehow, most people who read the above definition come to the erroneous conclusion that it does not encompass machines and buildings. As I am going to show later, this definition is exactly identical to the conventional definition, as far as machines and buildings are concerned. Why the use of the word *inventory* rather than the more understood term *assets?* It was done purposely to highlight the fact that this definition departs drastically from convention when referring to material inventory.

What value should we attach to a finished product stored in a warehouse? According to the definition given above, we are allowed to assign just the price that we paid to our vendors for the material and purchased parts that went into the product. There is no added value by the system itself, not even direct labor. This deviation certainly contradicts any conventional method of valuing inventory. It is not FIFO or LIFO or anything of that sort. Why the need for such a departure?

Added value. To what? To the product. But our concern is not the product, but rather the company. So what we actually have to ask ourselves is, "When is the only point in time that we add value to the company?" Only when we sell, not a minute before!! The whole concept of adding value to a product is a distorted local optimum. So we should not be surprised if it will cause distortions in the company's behavior. Let's examine some of the more common distortions.

Suppose you are the plant manager of a production plant that belongs to a large conglomerate. You are not in charge of sales and marketing, these functions are the responsibility of the division which, in your case, is located in a different state.

Last year, your plant made only one percent net profit. The bonus you received was so small that you needed a microscope to see it. You are under tremendous pressure from your wife to move to a larger house, and your oldest child has just entered an Ivy League school. You definitely need more money. You are determined to earn a hefty bonus this year.

The sales of your plant are forecasted to be exactly the same as last year. You can do nothing about it. The sales department, as we said, does not report to you. But corporate is signaling to you (if you can call a two-by-four a signal) that they consider reduction in inventory an extremely important performance measure. Lately, headquarters has come to realize that inventory is a liability. Inventory is under your control. So, this year you concentrated on reducing it, but not at the expense of the other performance of the company.

Your efforts have succeeded in cutting work-in-process and finished-goods inventories to half the beginning-of-the-year levels. You have achieved this without jeopardizing sales or customer service. As a matter of fact, you have improved customer service. Moreover, you have achieved these results without making other types of investments. You have not purchased any more equipment, nor have you installed a new sophisticated computer system. You did not even increase operating expense, or hire a herd of consultants to help you do the job. At the same time, you did not decrease operating expense either.

How did you achieve the reduction of inventory? Since sales were constant, you simply choked, for a while, purchase and production. Yes, your labor force was not fully utilized during that transition period, but you could not lay them off. If you did, not only would you have trouble with the union, you would have run the risk of not being able to rehire them. Your people are very good and do not have much of a problem finding other jobs. You are too experienced a plant manager to let them go, just to face, six weeks later, the need to retrain new hirees.

So let us summarize your performance. Sales and customer service were not jeopardized, investment in non-material did not increase, operating expense remained constant, but work-in-process and finished-goods inventory took a nice nose dive. Any manager would be proud of such results.

Oh, by the way, how much of a bonus did you get? Why are you now looking for a new job? Yes, many plant managers have found themselves in this enigmatic situation. They have done things that make sense, and all of a sudden are surprised when their financial statements condemn their actions. What will be the financial judgment on the case described above? Why did corporate instruct the plants to reduce inventory? Because inventory is a liability. But when they come to judge performance at the end of the year, under what heading do we find inventory on the financial statement? Under assets. Assets are the exact opposite of liabilities.

Reduce inventory, it is a liability. Ah, you have reduced it! Now we will change the rules. All of a sudden it is an asset, and the axe is coming down on your neck. Where is the actual difference hiding? Let's examine it a little bit more closely.

Inventory is recorded on our balance sheet as an asset, But at what value? As far as work-in-process and finished-goods are concerned, the value used is not just the raw material price, but also the value added to the product. When one chokes purchasing, what turns into cash is only the purchase price of the materials that were not bought. All the added value is not compensated, and thus it will appear in this year's bottom line result as a loss.

The local viewpoint of adding value to the product causes many companies to slow down considerably their efforts to reduce material inventory. The only time when a company can afford such an action is when sales rise enough to more than compensate for the negative impact of the inventory reduction. This phenomena is observed throughout the United States and Europe on a grand scale. No wonder. We should remember the impact of a distortion in the measurements.

TELL ME HOW YOU MEASURE ME, AND I WILL TELL YOU HOW I WILL BEHAVE. IF YOU MEA-SURE ME IN AN ILLOGICAL WAY . . . DO NOT COMPLAIN ABOUT ILLOGICAL BEHAVIOR.

The snake of the added-value concept also raises its ugly head in another way and causes even greater devastation. In the early eighties, there was an American company of about nine billion dollars in sales that ended the year with a small loss. It was after many years of profit, and it was totally unexpected.

You can imagine that Wall Street did not react in a favorable way. Shareholders were not exactly happy. In a surprisingly short time, the head of the CEO rolled, and a new, tough manager was hired to replace him.

The new CEO openly declared that he was not interested in all this humanitarian mumbo jumbo. He was interested in only one thing—the bottom line. The board of directors loved it, which was probably why they hired him. His first action, as the story goes, was to ask for a list of all the parts produced by the company. You can imagine the size of the computer print-out!

For each part he wanted to know EXACTLY how much it cost the company to produce it, and what the outside purchase price would be if it were possible to obtain it from a vendor. Then he put forth a mandatory policy; every part that is cheaper to buy on the outside—do not have any sentiments, we are here for business—immediately stop producing it and out-source. Of course, the necessary "adjustments" were to be made in the labor force.

Is your company generally making the same decision when-ever make-buy decisions are considered? However, in that case, it was done on a grand scale, totally focused, and expeditiously executed. No one was allowed to procrastinate. A few people who tried to delay the process were turned into "examples."

Four months later, the CEO asked for an updated list. Checking actual performance is very important in business. Once again the list of all parts that were still being produced was compiled, each with an updated internal cost and the updated purchase price. We all know what happened.

It is sometimes possible to fire people. It is much harder to lay off a machine. But did you ever try to fire a building, without using a match? Every part that remained now had to carry on its shoulders the costs that were previously shared with their "friends" that had now been out-sourced. Every single part became more expensive. So now, many more parts moved into the out-source category, since they were now more expensive to produce in-house than to purchase from the outside. Another huge wave of trimming took place.

Looks ridiculous? It's not so wild when we remember that most Western companies use the same concept, even though not on the same scale. Then, so the story continues, the fourth quarter arrived. The CEO was more than a little bewildered. His financial statements were not exactly glowing. The honeymoon period with the board and Wall Street was already over.

He made a quick assessment, and realized that the vast majority of the company's investment was in the final-assembly plants, so he decided to concentrate there. At least let's make the assembly plants as efficient as possible. What is their major excuse, lack of parts? We'll give them an ample supply. Being a realistic doer, he succeeded in getting loans from 204 banks. He used this money to make sure that all the assembly plants ran uninterrupted for three shifts a day, seven days a week, for the entire fourth quarter. Efficiencies reached levels never seen before. Of course, current orders could not sustain such a huge production rate, but there was no major difficulty in pulling forward from the long-term forecast. Another common practice in many Western companies.

At the end of that year, the financial statements totally justified the CEO's actions. A lot of overhead was absorbed, and the bottom-line results glittered. The CEO was rewarded generously, but that did not comfort him too much because he did not know how to proceed. So he just resigned. This story could have been just an interesting anecdote if it were not for its ramifications. The next year tens of thousands of people lost their jobs, the company shrank to one-third of its size and had to change its name. Can you name the company?

These are all common management practices—chasing not real profits, but artificial number-game profits. The added-value concept allows for the ridiculous notion of "inventory profits" and "inventory losses." Usually (but not always) companies stop the inventory profits game before their cash position is jeopardized beyond the point of no return. But this does not mean that damage is not done. Finished-goods distribution warehouses are filled to the brim, causing the company to be at a large time distance from its clients.

Many companies today are serving their clients through a distance of three to six months of finished-goods inventories in a world where their product life-cycle is less than two years. What happens to such a company if it competes against another company that, even though it produces on the other side of the globe, is only thirty days remote from the same market? Who will win in the long run? Who has already won in so many industries? Can these companies get rid of the inventory monkey on their backs? Only very slowly, considering today's investor mentality.

Top management will probably not be able to explain to their shareholders the devastating bottom line "results."

TELL ME HOW YOU MEASURE ME, AND I WILL TELL YOU HOW I WILL BEHAVE. IF YOU MEASURE ME IN AN ILLOGICAL WAY . . . DO NOT COMPLAIN ABOUT ILLOGICAL BEHAVIOR.

Let us not underestimate the impact this statement has on the viability of companies.

Taking added value out of inventory does not mean that we do not have these outlays of money. To account for them is the task of the third measurement—operating expense.

Operating expense is defined as all the money the system spends in turning INVENTORY into THROUGHPUT.

Again the phrase "all the money." Operating expenses are not just the money that we pay for direct labor. What is the job of a salesperson if not to turn inventory into throughput? What is the job of a foreman? What are the jobs of managers or their secretaries? Why do we differentiate between people who are doing exactly the same task, just because some of them happen to physically touch the products?

Notice the different words chosen in the last two definitions. *Invested* in inventory, *spent* for operating expense. In which category will you put the salaries of the engineers doing research and development?

To clarify even more the usage of these three definitions, let's fulfill our previous promise. We still have to show why we claimed that the above definition of inventory is totally in line with convention where machines and buildings are concerned. Consider for example a purchase of oil for lubricating machines. At the time of the purchase, we should not consider the money paid to the vendor as operating expense. We still own the oil. It is definitely inventory. Now we start to use the oil. The portion that we have used has to be moved from inventory and recategorized as operating expense. Just simple common sense.

Consider next the purchase of material. The money paid to the vendors is not operating expense, it is inventory. Now we process these materials in the attempt to convert them into throughput. While processing, some of the material is scrapped. The portion that is scrapped will have to be removed from inventory and categorized as operating expense.

Now consider the purchase of a new machine. The purchase price is not operating expense, since we still own the machine. It is inventory. As we use the machine, we are gradually scrap-ping it, so a portion of its value must, from time to time, be removed from inventory and be put into operating expense. What do we call the mechanism that is supposed to do this task? Depreciation.

6. *Measurements, Bottom Line, and Cost Accounting*

We have seen two very distinct differences between conventional measurements and the ones we have proposed here. Have we reached the core reason for our intuitive feelings that we are dealing with NEW OVERALL MANAGEMENT PHILOSOPHIES? As much as we would like to believe it, it unfortunately does not stand up under serious scrutiny. First of all, the above distinctions are made just by the Theory of Constraints. The other two movements, JIT and TQM, have not bothered to verbalize the fundamental measurements precisely, and are thus quite oblivious to such fine distinctions. Another reason is that the fundamental measurements of throughput, inventory, and operating expense are also used by our conventional management as well.

To prove this point, it is easy to demonstrate that every manager is very familiar with throughput, inventory, and operating Expense. Our familiarity is so great that it is a "no-brainer" to state the desired direction we want each measurement to move. Just ask yourself, "Do you want to increase or decrease throughput?" The answer is obvious: "We would like to increase the rate at which our company generates money."

Inventory. Increase or decrease? All will answer: "We would like to decrease the amount of money captured in our compa-

31

nies." And what about operating expense? It is so obvious that the question does not even deserve an answer.

Let's take it one step deeper. If we have three measurements, every action must be evaluated according to its impact on all three. That is why we have three measurements, and not just one. What is one of the most powerful ways to reduce operating expense? Fire everybody. Operating expense goes down gorgeously. Of course, throughput goes to hell, but who cares?

In evaluating any action, we must remember that we have three measurements, not just one. Otherwise, extremely devastating actions will be taken. This means that the final judge is not the measurements themselves, but the relationships between these measurements. Having three measurements implies, mathematically, two relationships. We can choose any two relationships, as long as all three measurements are involved. What popular choices do we already have? Consider, for example, the following relationship, throughput minus operating expense: $T - OE$. Does this relationship look familiar? Yes, you are right, this is our old friend, NET PROFIT.

What about the slightly more complicated relationship, throughput minus operating expense, divided by inventory: $(T - OE)/I$? This looks even more familiar. This is simply RETURN ON INVESTMENT.

There is nothing new in the fundamental measurements (T, I, OE), as can be clearly seen from the fact that they lead directly to the old and conventional bottom line judgments. So it looks as if we are stuck. If nothing is new in the goal, and nothing is new in the measurements, how can we justify the name NEW OVERALL MANAGEMENT PHILOSOPHY?

Before we dive into it, it might be interesting to remember that any two relationships of the three measurements can be used as final judge. Is another pair in practice today?

Consider for example, the straightforward ratios of throughput divided by operating expense (T/OE) and throughput divided by inventory (T/I). Can you attach names to these ratios? Yes, you are right, the first one is the conventional definition of PRODUCTIVITY, and the second we commonly refer to as TURNS.

We can use the pair NP and ROI, or the pair PRODUCTIVITY and TURNS. Take your pick. But unless you want to confuse yourself, do not use all four. Think carefully now about those people who are telling us authoritatively that we must have one measurement system for the macro, like NP and ROI, and another one for the micro, like PRODUCTIVITY and TURNS. What an absurd claim—especially when we are always aware of the fact that as long as we have one company having one goal we had better have just one financial system.

Where does cost accounting come into the picture, if at all? At first glance it looks as if it doesn't have a place. But that is not necessarily so. Cost accounting, when invented, was a stroke of genius that answered a very important need. Almost a mandatory one. To understand the role cost accounting is playing today, it might help if we took a more philosophical overview.

Cost accounting has fallen victim to a very generic process. Many companies are being victimized just because they haven't realized it. In the current fast-changing, competitive world, it is essential to be aware of this process, otherwise we will be paralyzed in more than one way. Somehow, most managers look desperately for anchors, for ultimate solutions. But ultimate solutions imply not only the ability to recognize "truth," but also unrealistically assume a constant and unchanging world. Ultimate solutions do not exist in reality; there are only powerful solutions.

A powerful solution addresses a very big problem. A solution, as good and elegant as it may be, can not be a powerful solution if it only addresses a trivial problem. A powerful solution is a definitive answer to a severe problem, a problem that impairs the overall performance of a company, a problem that distorts the behavior of many of its people, its managers, and their actions. Thus, implementing a powerful solution leads di-

rectly to a drastic impact in the company—a change in its behavior as well as its performance.

We should always keep before our eyes the fact that our organizations do not exist in a vacuum; our companies constantly
interact with their surroundings. When a company goes
through a significant change, it impacts its surroundings. As a
result, higher performance will be demanded. Implementing a
powerful solution causes a drastic change in a company. In turn
a change is triggered in its surroundings, creating new chal-
lenges which might make the original powerful solution obsolete.

We must come to terms with an unpleasant reality: the more
powerful the solution, the faster it might make itself obsolete.
Ignoring this reality leads to only one conclusion—THE POW-
ERFUL SOLUTION OF YESTERDAY MIGHT BECOME
THE DISASTER OF TODAY!

This is exactly what happened in the case of cost accounting.
In the next chapter, we will analyze to what extent, when invented, cost accounting was one of the most powerful solutions
in the history of industry. It was one of the major tools that
enabled industry to flourish and grow with remarkable speed.
Due to this growth, the need for better technology increased
exponentially. This same growth also provided the means to
finance the invention and development of technology. But as
technology advanced, it changed the ratios between the need for
human muscles and the need for human brains. Overhead factors of companies have grown in the last century from modest
ratios of 0.1, to the current situation, where most companies
have overhead factors of somewhere between five and eight.
The expense of direct labor at the time cost accounting was
invented was about tenfold bigger than overhead. Today, we are
rapidly approaching the time when it will be just one tenth of
overhead.

Cost accounting was a powerful solution. It did change the
behavior and performance of industrial companies. Industry in
turn impacted the overall technology. Then technology pulled
the rug out from underneath cost accounting; the assumptions

on which cost accounting was based are no longer valid. The powerful solution rendered itself obsolete. Many companies are already facing the disaster resulting from following an obsolete solution.

7. *Exposing the foundation of cost accounting*

We have defined three measurements. Are they the ones we need? Will these measurements enable us to judge the impact of a local decision on the overall goal? Intuitively we feel that they are appropriate, but let's face it, we have not even started to substantiate this claim.

Any attempt to judge a local decision immediately highlights the need to break down each measurement into its components. What components comprise the throughput of the company? The throughput of the company results from the sale of one type of product, plus a second type of product, etc. Products might also be services. So, the throughput of the company is just the summation of the throughput gained through the sales of all the individual products. In a more mathematical form:

$$T = \Sigma_p T_p$$

The same should be done for operating expense. We spend money in converting inventory to throughput. Who do we give this money to? To the workers and managers for their time, to the banks for interest, to the utility companies for energy, to Blue Cross/Blue Shield for medical insurance, and so on. There are many categories of expense. It should be noted that "prod-

36

ucts" are not one of these categories. Did you ever pay money to a product?

Likewise, it is important to note that vendors are not a category of operating expense. The money paid to vendors is not operating expense, but rather inventory. Thus, the total operating expense of a company is simply the summation of the individual categories of operating expenses. In a more mathematical form:

$$OE = \Sigma_c \, OE_c$$

The breakdown for inventory is obvious.

These breakdowns introduce a possible difficulty in using the measurements described above for a local decision. At the end, the final judges are NP and ROI. Now let's see what an awkward situation we are in. Net Profit is simply throughput minus operating expense. Mathematically it will take the form of:

$$NP = \Sigma_p T_p - \Sigma_c \, OE_c$$

Pay attention. The first summation is done on products, the second, on categories. If we try to add apples and oranges, fruit salad will be the result. So how are we going to handle the following important case? Suppose that we are evaluating the wisdom of launching a new product. We have a good guesstimate of how much we are going to sell. Our real interest lies not in launching the product but in the impact it will have on the net profit of the entire company.

How can we answer this question if we do not know the impact of launching the new product on the sales of the other products? How can we answer it if we do not know its impact on the various categories of operating expense? It might be that even though the throughput gained from this new product is quite high, our total net profit will go down. This is a very important decision, but even using the new measurements it doesn't look as if we can get a handle on local decisions.

Cost accounting was invented to answer such extremely important questions. The genius that invented it probably went through the following logical reasoning. He probably said, "I cannot answer your questions precisely, but there is no need to answer them precisely. In any case, the answer will be based on your guesstimate of how much of this new product we are going to sell. What I must do is provide a very good approximation, and this I can do."

His solution attempted to simplify the situation by the move from apples and oranges to apples and apples, from two different breakdowns—product and expense categories—to just one. He probably said, "I can find an alternative breakdown of operating expense, not by categories, but by products. Yes, it will not be accurate, but it will be a good enough approximation."

All we have to do is change the question that led to the breakdown of operating expense. Rather than asking the standard question of our P&L, "To whom do we pay money?" let's ask, "Why do we pay money?" Why do we pay money to a worker? Because we have decided to produce a particular product. Thus, we can at least split the direct labor category product by product.

Let's remember, when cost accounting was invented at the beginning of this century, in most companies direct labor was paid according to pieces produced. Unlike today, where we pay by hours spent in the plant, and where we have many reasons (not just unions) to shy away from the hire-fire mentality.

What about other categories of expense where a split by product is impossible? For example, we certainly do not pay the president a salary because of a decision to produce a particular product. Let's lump all these other expenses together, preferably under a name that has a negative connotation. What do you think about a name like "overhead," or even better, "burden"? This name certainly demonstrates our disgust with expenses that do not fall neatly into the desired product by product split. Yes, we do run a risk in calling all managers "burden," but hopefully they will not notice.

Putting jokes aside, what should we do with all those "overhead" expenses? The person who invented cost accounting didn't hesitate. Remember, at the beginning of the century all these expenses were extremely small compared with direct labor. He had already dealt with the dominant bulk. So, his suggestion was straightforward: "Spread all those expenses according to the contribution of direct workers." ALLOCATION was invented.

What did he gain by this trick? He was able to split operating expense by products, exactly the same way throughput was split. Now we can move to the next step, since we have apples with apples. The mathematical presentation takes a much simpler form:

$$NP = \Sigma_p\, T_p - \Sigma_p OE_p$$
$$NP = \Sigma_p (T - OE)_p$$

This is a huge achievement. The approximation suggested by cost accounting enabled us to dissect a company into product by product classes. Now, we can make decisions regarding one product, without looking at all the others.

This innovation was extremely powerful. It enabled companies to grow in size while proliferating the product range. It is interesting to note that among the first to adopt cost accounting were Du Pont and General Motors. It was not recognized by Ford, who limited himself to just one main product.

But now the situation is a little bit different. The advance of technology changed industry to the extent that both fundamental assumptions of cost accounting are no longer valid. Direct labor is no longer paid by pieces produced, but by the mere fact that the workers took on themselves the obligation to come to work. Overhead no longer represents a tiny fraction of operating expense, but rather it is larger than direct labor expenses.

Today, the entire financial community has awakened both to the fact that cost accounting is no longer applicable, and that something must be done. Unfortunately, they are not going back to the fundamentals, the financial statements logic, and seeking there answers for these important business questions.

Instead, the financial community is totally immersed in an attempt to save the obsolete solution.

"Cost drivers" and "activity-based costing" are the names of these fruitless efforts. It is evident that we can no longer allocate according to direct labor. So, their way is to say: some expenses we can allocate at the unit level, others only at the batch level, others at the product level, still others at the product group level, and some only at the company level. Yes, the allocation can be done in this way. But for what purpose? Anyhow, we cannot aggregate them at the unit level, or even at the product level. So why play all these number games?

Remember, allocation was invented in order to move from two different splits, products and categories, to one single split. The whole purpose was to reach one classification, enabling a dissection of the company, so we could make better decisions. Now under the name of allocation, rather than shrinking the number of classifications, we inflate them. We fell in love with a technique. We forgot the purpose—to be able to judge the impact of any local decision on the bottom line.

We are now at a crossroads. We can continue to explore how the fundamental measurements can be used for local decisions, and develop an alternative solution to the problem that cost accounting is unable to solve anymore; or, we can continue to examine what is "new" in the new overall management philosophies; or, we can expose the damage that using the now erroneous approximation of cost accounting causes to companies all over the Western world. All three avenues are important. All three must be dealt with. But since attacking cost accounting brings joy to so many functions in a company, why don't we continue with that issue first.

8. *Cost accounting was the traditional measurement*

The problem of getting rid of cost accounting does not lie in the financial community, but with the management of other functions. The practitioners of cost accounting gladly give it up when they see a logical, practical alternative presented to them. They, more than anyone else, know to what extent cost accounting does not really work.

Talk with any controllers, and listen to their complaints. They will tell you that they compile the numbers in the only way they know. Then, other managers make decisions, seemingly based on these numbers. If they would just have asked, the controller would have told them that their decision has nothing to do with the compiled numbers. What makes financial people furious is the fact that after this, these managers have the gall to blame them for their decisions. The cry of the controllers is, "Give us a better way!" No, the problem certainly does not lie with the financial people. The ones who do not want to give up cost accounting are the managers, in production, design, purchasing, distribution, and definitely sales. Why are they so attached to this dinosaur?

The only way that I can explain it, is to recognize that cost accounting has brought with it its own nomenclature. We have all been born into a world where this nomenclature has become

41

a part of our reality. Let's examine the following mathematical creature: "operating expense of a product"—the outcome of allocation. This is certainly just a mathematical phantom. We have never paid money to a product. Nevertheless, we have a name for it today. We call it **PRODUCT COST.**

If we no longer accept the approximation of cost accounting, we have to be consistent and erase its nomenclature. Product cost exists only when we accept the approximation. In the original formula—throughput minus operating expense (the base of our P&L formula)—cost of categories exists, but not the cost of products. Try to imagine what would happen if the term "product cost" was wiped out. Every design engineer would probably commit hara-kiri. They would lose the yardstick that guides them in the final stages of design. But "product cost" is not the only term that has come with cost accounting. Look on its resulting formula:

$$NP = \Sigma_p(T - OE)_p$$

The expression "Throughput minus the operating expense of a product," which we call net profit of a product, is definitely just a mathematical phantom. Net profit exists only for the company, not for the product. This means that all the following terms, product profit, product margin, and product cost, must be omitted from our vocabulary the minute that the approximation is recognized to be no longer valid. Just try to imagine a salesman's expression when he finds out that these terms can no longer be part of his vocabulary.

Unfortunately, these terms have very deep roots in our decision process. We still use them even in those cases where we can make the decision using the original P&L formula more easily, much better, and without any approximation. Let's explore just two typical examples out of the multitude that exist.

Every conglomerate in the United States and in Europe reports its performance according to the original formula: total throughput minus total operating expenses. Nevertheless, if you dive into these same conglomerates, to the division level, and certainly to the plant level and down, you will find another mechanism. You will find the diabolic creature called BUDGETS. What is a budget? It is just the construction of the original P&L formula through the approximation. The construction of the net profit for the plant through the "net profit" of the individual products. Of course, it does not match. So we call the mismatch "variance," and now it matches!

What comes out of this awkward method? Just go into a plant toward the end of the month, when everybody is climbing the walls, and try to find the plant manager—it won't be easy! The plant manager is hiding with the controller in a remote room, trying, somehow, to straighten out the numbers. The end result is that after all this mammoth work, we really don't know if the plant made or lost money this month. It depends on some allocation done months ago.

Is there any problem in calculating net profit in a straightforward way, the same way it is done for the entire conglomerate? Certainly not. It is much, much faster and requires much less data. That's all. So why do we do it the hard way, just to get the wrong answer? It looks like the tendency to use "product cost" and "product profit" is almost compulsory. Can you find another reason?

Is time and effort wasted the only damage done? No, it goes much deeper. Suppose that you have taken a correct action that really improved your plant. But your P&L, calculated by the variance technique, has shown for two or three months in a row that the situation is deteriorating. You will probably reverse the correct action. Measuring performance has a huge impact on behavior.

The saddest part of it all is to see a small business growing nicely under an entrepreneur. Then the business reaches the level where much better financial control is needed. The entrepreneur hires a financial professional; sometimes this professional has worked at the plant level for a conglomerate. This person brings with him the variance technique, and the entrepreneur loses the handle on his business.

But let's examine another case where the cost-accounting

type of thinking is used extensively, even though the straight-forward P&L formula is sufficient. Suppose a company is considering the opposite question of the one that triggered the invention of cost accounting. Not launching a new product, but whether or not to drop existing products.

This type of exercise is done usually at the corporate level. What are the first candidates to be considered at that level? Yes, they are the least profitable products, the losers, the dogs. Have you noticed that we are already using cost-accounting terminology?

How is the calculation done? Usually the first question asked is: "How much is the throughput of the product?" No problem, just the selling price minus the price of the raw materials. The next question, of course, is: "How much does it cost to produce this product?" We would like to know how much profit we make on this item. Once again, no real problem. At corporate, we just look to see how much direct labor is needed to make this product. Twelve point seven-three minutes. At corporate they know everything to an accuracy of at least four digits. At the plant we do not really know if it takes ten or fifteen minutes, but at corporate, they know everything. Then, we convert this time into dollars using the labor rate and multiply the result by the overhead factor; a factor that was calculated based on last year's/quarter's realities, even though we are now trying to change something. Never mind. Now we have the cost.

What happens when the cost is too close to the throughput? Or even worse, higher? The order to stop producing and marketing the product is almost immediately sent to the plant. The plant personnel usually rebel. "We have enough experience. We have already been burned more than once by the domino effect. Today, they will trim this product. The overhead is not going to go down. Then, three months later, another whiz-kid in corporate will do the same calculation, and we will lose two more products. And shortly, the plant will face the threat of being closed."

Yet it is so easy to do the right calculation using the original P&L formula: total throughput minus total operating expense.

First we have to ask ourselves the following: "If we drop this product, what will be the impact on the total throughput?" We know the answer, up to the extent that we can rely on the sales forecast—in reality nothing is totally precise. We are going to lose the sales of this particular product.

Secondly, what impact will dropping this product have, not on "cost," but on the total operating expense? According to our definition of operating expense, this last question basically asks: "How many people are we going to lay off? In production? In dispatching? In engineering? In accounting? And please, specify names!" Somehow, an estimation of "we are going to lay off twenty people" shrinks to six or seven when we stop dealing with numbers and start dealing with real people.

How many people are we going to lay off? Nobody? We are just going to move them to another department? I have a surprise for you. Have you noticed that moving people from one department to another somehow does not affect the operating expense of the company? Ahhh, you say that they are now going to be more productive in their new positions? Notice, that whenever we are unsure, we just switch terminology. From profit to productivity, for example. What do you mean by productive? The throughput of other products will go up? Which one, and by how much? If we do not know, how can we use it as an argument?

By trimming a particular product, how much will the total operating expense go down? How many people are we going to lay off? It is an unpleasant question, but not one that is hard to answer. If the resulting reduction in throughput is less than the reduction in operating expense, let's drop the product. Otherwise, we are making a decision that jeopardizes reaching the company's goal.

Using this straightforward method, we sometimes find that it does not make sense to drop one particular product or another particular product, but it does make sense to drop both of them together. We cannot lay off half a person. But we can lay off a whole one. It is about time to realize that in the conventional way of "product cost," we are trying to "save" seven percent of a machine, and thirteen percent of a worker. It is time to come back to reality.

How many businesses has U.S. industry lost in the last twenty years to Mexico and the Philippines because of this awkward way of calculation? Even today, conglomerates are moving products from one plant to the other because of such reasoning. "It is too expensive to produce this product in this plant, the overhead is too high. We'll move it to another plant." "Are you going to fire anybody in the first plant?" "Of course not! We have a long-term agreement with the union." "And what about the other plant?" "Oh, over there, we will have to hire a few more people, but they are cheap labor."

"Product cost," "product margin," and "product profit," have turned into the basic language of industrial enterprises. Using cost accounting has almost forced the classification of the entire business to be a "by product" classification. The above examples just highlight the type of mistakes that we are making. They just highlight what fights face any manager who dares to use intuition or common sense. The devastating ramifications reach every aspect of the business. Maybe the best way to summarize this chapter is by repeating a short story from the book *Made in Japan,* written by Akio Morita, the president of Sony.

When Sony was just a very small company, Mr. Morita was offered a big order by an American company, which had a chain of 150 stores. He had to submit a price proposal for quantities of 5,000, 10,000, 30,000, 50,000, and 100,000. The best way is to let you read his common-sense considerations directly in his book, but here is the response of the American company's purchasing manager upon receiving his quotes: "Mr. Morita, I have worked as a purchasing manager for close to thirty years, but you are the first person who ever told me that as I buy more, the price per unit is going up. It is illogical." A typical response of cost accounting to P&L reasoning.

9. *The new measurements' scale of importance*

Let's review where we are. We are still trying to find what led our intuition to choose this very demanding phrase of NEW OVERALL MANAGEMENT PHILOSOPHY. We verbalized the goal, at least as far as public business enterprises are concerned, and we could not find anything new. Then we dove into this stormy subject of measurements, just to realize that even though this subject certainly needs some cleanup, basically, nothing is new. Throughput, inventory, and operating expense were known and used much before the new movements.

The only anchor, the only hint, that we still have is the invalidity of cost accounting. Maybe something is distorted in the way we relate to the measurements. Can it be that what is new is not the measurements themselves, but the scale of importance in which we regard them? Is there any conventional scale of importance? It certainly is not formally stated, but is there in practice such a conventional scale? Let's try to approach it systematically.

The final judges, as we have said so many times, are Net Profit and Return on Investment. Throughput and operating expense impact both of these items, while inventory impacts only the latter. This naturally places throughput and operating expense on a more important level than inventory. What about the relationship between throughput and operating expense? At first glance, it looks as though both are of equal importance, since the bottom line is impacted by the difference between them. But this is not actually so. We are accustomed to place more importance on something that looks more tangible. Let's remind ourselves that in conventional management thinking, operating expense is considered more tangible than throughput. Throughput depends on external factors that we do not control —on our clients and our markets. Operating expense is much better known, much more under our control. Thus, our natural tendency is to place operating expense on a slightly higher level than throughput.

We have to be careful, while evaluating the conventional scale of importance, not to be influenced by the winds of change of the eighties. Let's not allow ourselves, at this stage, to distort the analysis of the conventional scale just because our intuitive belief, that throughput is dominant, has been intensified in the last five or so years. Especially now, when we have to look at our realities courageously.

In any company, the most dominant measurements are not the bottom-line measurements. They are dominant only at the very thin layer of top management. But just dive down the pyramid, and the measurements rapidly dissolve into more and more cost-accounting-type measurements. What is "cost?" Just a synonym for operating expense. All cost procedures are thus geared to attach a value to actions impacting operating expense. As a result, actions that have their dominant effect on throughput will be classified as intangibles.

Consider, for example, actions that have their major impact on improving customer service, or on shrinking production lead time; such actions are advocated today by top management as extremely important. Nevertheless, if we want to invest in equipment to achieve those results, and this equipment does not also reduce costs, the middle-level managers are in a very awkward situation. When they fill out the appropriation request for the needed equipment, they must justify it under the title of intangible. We have come to learn that intangible is certainly not synonymous with unimportant. Intangible is just an expression we use when we cannot attach a numeric value. Cost accounting forces this title on any action that is geared toward increasing future throughput. "Cost," being almost synonymous with operating expense, is totally blind in the direction of throughput.

In spite of efforts by top management, operating expense is considered to be far more tangible than throughput, placing it as a dominant first on the scale of importance. Throughput trails far behind. Just look at what banks and other lenders demand when a company has to submit a recovery plan. Trimming—reduction of operating expense—is mandatory.

What about inventory? Due to the awkward concept of added value to the product, reducing inventory impairs, rather than improves, the bottom line; inventory is left to be a very distant third on the scale. The conventional scale of importance is thus: operating expense first, throughput a mere second, and inventory a very remote third. This scale of importance is, for the new movements, like a red cape to a bull. They all go zealously out of their way to attack and condemn this scale.

Let's clarify for ourselves the scale of importance of our measurements that all three movements, JIT, TOC, and TQM, are recommending. All three movements have one dominant phrase in common. Talk with the disciples of any one of them, and you will hear the same song: "A process of ongoing improvement." As a matter of fact, we should have had this motto a long time ago. Remember, the goal of the company is not just to make money, it is to make MORE money, now as well as in the future. A process of ongoing improvement stems directly from the goal's definition.

If a process of ongoing improvement is what we are after, which one of the three avenues of throughput, inventory, or operating expense is more promising? If we just think for a minute the answer becomes crystal clear. Both inventory and operating expense we strive to decrease. Thus, both of them offer only a limited opportunity for ongoing improvement. They are both limited by zero.

This is not the case with the third measurement, throughput. We strive to increase throughput. Throughput does not have any intrinsic limitation; throughput must be the cornerstone of any process of ongoing improvement. It must be first on the scale of importance.

Now what about inventory and operating expense; which one of these two is more important? At first glance, our prior analysis looks flawless. Operating expense impacts both bottom-line measurements, whereas inventory impacts only one of them directly. But this cannot possibly be a decisive argument, since our choice of the final judges (NP and ROI) was arbitrary. If we had chosen the alternative pair, productivity and turns, this argument would fall flat on its face.

The basic flaw in placing operating expense above inventory stems from the fact that we took into account just the DIRECT impact of inventory, not its INDIRECT impact. The conventional body of knowledge was totally concentrated on operating expense, and thus recognized only one indirect channel of inventory—the way inventory impacts the bottom line through operating expense. If we will refer to the machine portion of inventory, this indirect channel is called depreciation. If we refer to the material portion of the inventory, it is called carrying cost.

All three new movements have recognized the existence of another considerably more important indirect channel, the indirect channel by which inventory—especially the time-related portion of it—impacts future throughput. In the book *The Race,* which is totally devoted to the subject of inventory, Robert Fox and I devoted over thirty pages to describe and prove this indirect channel. *The Race* clearly shows that inventory almost determines the future ability of a company to compete in its markets. This indirect impact turns out to be so important that all three movements have placed inventory second on the scale of importance, leaving operating expense to be a close third.

The new scale of importance is thus totally different from the conventional one. Throughput is dominant. Inventory is second. Operating expense has been tumbled from its lofty position to a modest third place.

The impact that this new scale of importance has on every decision that management makes is staggering. Many actions that make perfect sense under the conventional scale become totally absurd when viewed from this new angle. That is why all three movements have gone out of their way to preach what seem to be just common-sense trivialities.

Theory Of Constraints hammers over and over again: "Local optima do not add up to the optimum of the total." Total Quality Management reminds us that: "It is not enough to do things right. What is more important is to do the right things." And Just In Time puts on its flag: "Do not do what is not needed."

10. *The resulting paradigm shift*

What actually happened when we deposed operating expense as king of the mountain, and replaced it with throughput? The realization of the magnitude of the change required is just now starting to emerge. It is actually the switch from viewing our organizations as systems of independent variables to viewing them as systems of dependent variables. This is the biggest switch any scientist can imagine.

Let's try to digest it, stripping away the scientific "glamour." Ask yourself, "How many outlets of operating expense exist in a company?" Every worker is an outlet, every engineer, salesman, clerk, or manager is an outlet of operating expense. Every bit of scrap, every place where we consume energy is an outlet of operating expense. This is a world where almost everything is important. This is the "cost world."

Of course, not everything is important to the same degree. Some things are more important than the others. Even in the cost world, we recognize the Pareto principle, the 20–80 rule. Twenty percent of the variables are responsible for 80 percent of the end result. But this rule is statistically correct only when we are dealing with a system of independent variables. The "cost world" gives the perception that our organization is actually such a system—that the outlets of operating expense are hardly connected. Money leaks from many, many small and big holes.

Now, look at the picture when throughput becomes dominant in our perception. Many functions have to carry out, in synch, many tasks, until a sale is realized, until throughput is gained. The "throughput world" is a world of dependent variables.

In the throughput world, even the Pareto principle must be understood in a totally different manner. It is no longer the 20–80 rule. It is much closer to the 0.1–99.9 rule. A tiny fraction (0.1 percent) of the variables determines 99.9 percent of the result. Looks strange? Almost unbelievable? Just remind yourself what you have known all along. We are dealing here with "chains" of actions. What determines the performance of a chain? "The strength of the chain is determined by the strength of its WEAKEST link." How many weakest links exist in a chain?. As long as statistical fluctuations prevent the links from being totally identical, there is only one weakest link in a chain.

What is an appropriate name for the concept of the weakest link, the link that limits the overall strength (performance) of the chain? A very appropriate name is CONSTRAINT. How many constraints exist in a company? That depends on how many independent chains exist. It cannot be too many. It is not just products that create chains, combining different types of resources to each other. It is also resources that create chains, combining different products with each other.

In our organizations, the proper analogy would be a grid, rather than a chain. In any event, there is an immense amount of interactions between the variables. These interactions, coupled with statistical fluctuations, are an almost dominating factor in every organization, and this precludes an organization from having many constraints. In real life, 0.1–99.9 is probably an underestimation.

Are most of our managers managing according to the focusing process that is mandatory in the throughput world? The answer, unfortunately, is definitely not. Most of them complain that they have to devote more than 50 percent of their time to putting out fires. They are certainly "cost world" managers. Everything, or at least 20 percent of everything, is important.

Their attention is spread much too thin, on too many seemingly equally important problems.

Some managers even complain that they view themselves as immersed in a swimming pool filled with Ping-pong balls, and they must try to hold all the balls under water. If all balls have to be under water, if everything is important, then the realization of "throughput world" has not yet impacted these managers.

JIT and TQM are not helping much in stimulating the needed change. Yes, they are very active in forcing management to shift to the new scale of importance, but they have not done much to help management change to the new style required to cope with this new scale.

TQM, realizing that throughput is so important, has changed management's perception about the actions that must be taken. If it were not for TQM, customer service and product quality, subjects which are vitally important to increase future throughput, would not be at the top of their agenda, as they are today.

If it were not for JIT, inventory would still be considered an asset. The importance of shrinking production lead time, of reducing batches and set-up time, of improving preventive maintenance, would not be recognized. All those actions that lead to faster response to the market, all those actions that are essential to guarantee future throughput, would not have reached the board rooms.

What both TQM and JIT have failed to realize are the ramifications of the "throughput world"—the focusing that stems directly from the realization that we are dealing with interactive variables environments. How can it be that it is important to adhere to every detail of the product design specification (especially when nobody knows if the specified tolerances should be there in the first place)? How can it be that it is important to reduce set-up times on all machines? Or to have the highest reliability on all resources? These are concepts that are erroneously extrapolated from the previous "cost world" picture.

The situation today is quite appalling. On one hand, we have come to realize that so many drastic changes are needed, and on the other hand we are not guided by the accompanying focusing process. It starts to look as if many companies don't get enough excitement from "The End of the Month Syndrome" so they have added to it what can only be called "The Beginning of the Quarter New Improvement Project."

And what about cost accounting? TQM was just irritated by it, irritated by the fact that the investment in improving quality, which is done for the sake of the very important throughput gains, has to be justified by a much less important cost consideration. They simply solved their problem by shoving aside the financial measurements, stating that "Quality is Job One."

JIT has done basically the same thing. When I met Dr. Ohno, the inventor of KANBAN, the JIT system of Toyota, he told me that cost accounting was the one thing that he had to fight against all his life. "It was not enough to chase out the cost accountants from the plants, the problem was to chase cost accounting from my people's minds."

We must explore the ramifications that stem from a totally new perception of our realities, a perception in which very few things are really important. What must be changed by switching from the "cost world" to the "throughput world"? But before doing exactly that, we shouldn't forget that we have left behind a huge unsolved problem. As long as the goal of our company is to make money now as well as in the future, financial measurements are essential; we cannot proceed without them. Dropping cost accounting will leave us without a numerical way to judge many types of decisions. This leaves the door wide open for non-financial measurements, and they are already creeping in.

JIT is wrong in ignoring this issue. TQM is even worse, because it encourages non-financial measurements. Remember that one of the foundations of running an organization is the ability to judge the impact of a local decision on the bottom line. Try to measure by three or more non-financial measurements, and you have basically lost all control. Non-financial measurements are equivalent to anarchy. You simply cannot compare apples, oranges, and bananas, and you definitely cannot relate them to the bottom line! The goal is to make money. Every measurement must, by definition, have the dollar sign in it.

Let's remind ourselves that condemning the solutions that cost accounting brought might be very important, but this action on its own does not provide a solution to the problem. The original problem still exists. How can we judge the impact of a suggested decision? How, for example, can we judge whether or not we should launch a new product? What will be the impact on the bottom line?

Let's try to address this problem. Suppose that we are dealing with the question of launching a new product when we have an excess of everything. We have excess market, excess clients, excess resources. When this is the situation, what impact will launching a new product have on the sales of the other products? No impact whatsoever.

What impact will the launching of the new product have on operating expense? In the above case, no impact, if we have excess resources of each skill anyway, resources that we are paying for already.

When will the launching of a new product have an impact on other things? When we do not have enough. If we do not have enough market and we launch a new product, geared to the same clients and satisfying the same needs that our other products are satisfying, then we must expect a reduction of sales in those other products.

If the new product needs a resource that does not have enough capacity, then the only way we can provide this product to the market is either by reducing the offering of the other products, or by increasing investments and operating expenses to provide more capacity from that resource.

In summary, the only time that we are really facing a problem, the only time that launching a new product does have an impact on other things, is when there is something that we do not have enough of. What do we call something that we do not have enough of, to the extent that it limits the performance of the overall company? An appropriate name will be CON-STRAINT. Once again, the same word.

In the "throughput world," constraints are the essential classification, replacing the role that products played in the "cost world." It looks as though continuing to explore the ramifications of the "throughput world" may also solve the problem of finding a replacement for cost accounting.

11. *Formulating the Throughput World's decision process*

"Focus on everything, and you have not actually focused on anything." Focusing means: "Under my responsibility, I have this big area. I elect to concentrate most of my attention on a small fraction of it." Spreading attention equally to all portions of the area means no concentration whatsoever, no focusing.

In the "cost world," focusing is very hard to do. At best we have to focus on a very big portion of the details. This is not the case in the "throughput world." What should be the first step? Where should we concentrate? That is totally obvious, isn't it? On the weakest links, on the constraints. They are the ones that determine the overall performance of the company.

In light of the above, what would you suggest should be the first step? Yes, it is clear, we must first of all find the constraints of the system.

Are we guaranteed, in any case, to find something? In other words, is it mandatory that every system must have at least one constraint? Maybe the answer will be clearer if we ask the same question using different words; have you ever seen a company with no constraints whatsoever? The intuitive answer is obvious —never. In any chain, there must be one weakest link. But let's try to substantiate it a little further. If there is a company with no constraints, what does this mean? That nothing limits its performance. What must be the performance of this company? What must be its Net Profit and ROI? Infinite. Have you ever seen, or heard of, a company with infinite net profit?

The conclusion is obvious: every system must have at least one constraint. On the other hand, every system, in reality, must have a very limited number of constraints. Thus, the first focusing step of the Theory Of Constraints is intuitive:

1. Identify the System's Constraint(s)

(Put the *S* in the word *constraints* in parentheses, because there might be a system that has only one constraint.)

Identifying a constraint means that we already have some appreciation of the magnitude of its impact on the overall performance. Otherwise, we might also have some trivialities in the list of constraints, or as I call them, some choopchicks.

Is it important to prioritize them according to their impact? Not necessarily so. First of all, let's remember that at this stage, we do not have precise estimates. The second thing to remember is that the number of constraints is very, very limited. We have to handle all of them anyhow, so let's not waste time with fruitless effort. Identifying the constraints, that is what counts.

What should be our next step? We have just identified the constraints. We have found those points, those things, that we don't have enough of, to the extent that they limit the overall performance of our entire system. How should we manage them?

The intuitive response is to get rid of them. But you know as well as I that to get rid of a constraint sometimes takes a lot of time. For example, if the constraint is the market, to break this constraint might take many months, or even a year. Or, if the constraint is a machine, and we have decided to buy another one, the delivery time might be over six months. What are we going to do in the meantime? Sit around and do nothing? That does not seem like good advice for a second step.

How should we manage the constraints, the things that we

do not have enough of? At least, let's not waste them. Let's squeeze the maximum out of them. Every drop counts. To put it in a more civilized form, the second step of the Theory Of Constraints is thus:

2. Decide How to Exploit the System's Constraint(s)

Exploit simply means to squeeze the maximum out of them. I have deliberately chosen a word with slightly negative connotations. EXPLOIT, no matter what it takes. Let's understand something—I do not believe that in a company that loses money, we can have job security. In a company that loses money, job security is threatened no matter what the top management says. Here are the constraints, the ones that limit the overall performance. The job security of everyone in the company depends on the performance of these points. No mercy, squeeze the maximum out of them.

For example, let's suppose that the constraint is the market. There is enough capacity, but not enough orders. Then, exploit the constraint means: 100 percent on-time delivery. Not 99 percent, one hundred! If the market is the constraint, let's not waste anything.

Okay, we have now decided how we are going to manage the constraints. What about managing the vast majority of the company's resources which are, by definition, non-constraints? Should we leave them alone? Within a very short period of time they will stop working properly, and their actual availability will shrink to the extent that they will become constraints. How should we manage them?

The answer is intuitively obvious. In the previous step, we decided on a course of action that will yield the maximum that we can get under the current situation, but to achieve it the constraints need to consume things. If the non-constraints do not supply what the constraints need to consume, the above decision will just stay on paper; it will never be executed.

Should we encourage non-constraints to supply more than the constraints can absorb? This will not help anyone. On the contrary, it will hurt. Thus the non-constraints should supply everything the constraints need to consume, but not more. Let's write the third step of the focusing process:

3. Subordinate Everything Else to the Above Decision

Now we are in a state where we are managing the current situation. Is it the final step? Of course not. Constraints are not an act of God, we can do something about them. Now is the time to do what we were tempted to do before. Let's open the constraints. If we do not have enough, it does not mean that we cannot add. The next step is intuitively obvious.

4. Elevate the System's Constraint(s)

Elevate means "Lift the restriction." This is the fourth step, not the second step. So many times we have witnessed a situation where everybody was complaining about a huge constraint, but when they exercised the second step of exploitation, of just not wasting what was available, it turned out that there was more than enough. So let's not hastily run to approve subcontracting, or launch a fancy advertising campaign, etc. When the second and third steps are complete and we still have a constraint, that is the time to move to the fourth step—unless we are talking about crystal-clear cases, where the constraint is out of proportion to everything else.

By the fourth step, we have also taken care of the issue of moving the company forward. Can we stop here, or must we add a fifth step? The answer is once again intuitively obvious. If we elevate the constraint, if we add more and more to the things that we didn't have enough of, there must come a time when we do have enough. The constraint is broken. The performance of the company will rise, but will it jump to infinity? Obviously not. The performance of the entire company will be restricted by something else. The constraint has moved. Thus the fifth step is:

5. If, in the Previous Steps, a Constraint Has Been Broken, Go Back to Step One.

But this is not the entire fifth step. We must add to it a very big warning. You see, the constraint impacts the behavior of every other resource in the company. Everything must be subordinated to the constraint's maximum level of performance. Thus, from the existence of the constraint, we in the company derive many rules—sometimes formally, many times just intuitively. Now a constraint has been broken. It turns out, that in most cases, we do not bother to go back and examine those rules. They stay behind. Now, we have POLICY constraints. Thus, the fifth step must be expanded to:

5. If, in the Previous Steps, a Constraint Has Been Broken, Go Back to Step One, but Do Not Allow Inertia to Cause a System's Constraint.

I cannot exaggerate the importance of this added warning. In most companies that I have analyzed, I have not found physical constraints. I have found policy constraints. I have never seen a company which has a market constraint. I have seen many that have marketing policy constraints. It is very rare to see a company with a true capacity constraint, a true bottleneck, but very often we see companies with production and logistical policy constraints. This is, by the way, the case described in *The Goal*. Was the oven a capacity constraint? Did Alex Rogo buy a new oven? Not at all. He just changed some internal production and logistical policies. Before long capacity was coming out of his ears.

Except for two cases I have not seen vendor constraints, even though most companies complain about their vendors. However, I have seen devastating purchasing policy constraints.

It is very significant that every time that we dive to find the reasons for these awkward policies (and sometimes to tell the truth, we almost have to launch an archaeological dig), we find out that thirty years ago or so, when these particular policies were put into practice, they made perfect sense. All the reasons are long gone, but the policies are still with us.

Five steps—an intuitively obvious and simple procedure of focusing. Everybody knew them before, everybody understands that they ring true. No wonder, as our intuition stems from our real world experience, and our real world is the throughput world. Nevertheless, do managers really use these steps? In cases of emergencies, maybe. But otherwise? The grip of "Cost World" training is too strong. In spite of our clear common-sense intuition, our actions are much more directed by the formal "Cost World" procedures than the straightforward, totally obvious, five focusing steps of the "Throughput World."

12. *What is the missing link?—building a decisive experiment*

We took my advice, we spent hours and dozens of pages to find out what was new in the NEW OVERALL MANAGEMENT PHILOSOPHIES. Fine, but where does it leave us? It looks as if we have not even taken one small step toward the real issue. How can we design an information system?

So let's leave this "detour" and go back to the heart of our problem. Let's start with the question that every manager typically claims cannot be answered because of lack of information.

The goal of the company is to make more money now as well as in the future. How much net profit will our company make next quarter? Isn't this one of the more important questions? No, we do not want an estimation, we want a precise answer, to, let's say, plus or minus two cents. Can we answer it? No, there is not enough information. That is the usual answer.

What prevents us from answering precisely how much net profit we are going to make next quarter? Oh, many things. For example, we do not know how reliable our sales forecast is. And our firm orders are not exactly firm. Our clients have a tendency from time to time to change their minds. What are we going to do, sue them?

But the problem is not just with marketing information. We might also have many problems internally. Nobody guarantees that a machine will not break down—as a matter of fact, we can guarantee that a machine will go down, the only questions are which machine, when, and for how long? Our vendors are not totally reliable, many times they do not deliver on time, or they send the wrong quantities. Sometimes a whole shipment, when it arrives, turns out to be defective. I do not know about you, but our work force is not exactly super reliable, we have absenteeism problems. We have scrap, partly because of the process, partly because of the workers. And our foremen are not totally disciplined—we tell them what to do, they know much better. The list can go on, and on, and on. Is it lack of information? It sounds more like a list of complaints:

Clients change their minds.
Unreliable vendors.
Unreliable processes.
Unreliable machines.
Untrained work force.
Undisciplined management.

Looking on this list, there is something that starts to really bother us. We all know the sign of an excuse. A sign of an excuse is, "It's someone else's fault." Have you noticed what is common to this list? Yes. "Somebody else is responsible." The clients, the vendors, the machines, the work force . . . We are perfect, they are to be blamed. Don't you too smell a rat?

Is this a list of reasons why we cannot answer the question, "How much net profit are we going to make next quarter?" or is it really just a list of excuses? This is a very important question, because when we review this list, we see that it is a very good summary of the efforts we are currently making to improve our company.

We are trying hard to improve our sales forecast. Major efforts are made to improve relationships with our clients, and we have a very extensive program entitled "Vendor Program." As for our machines, we have embarked aggressively on preventive maintenance, and have also invested heavily in new equipment to improve reliability. As for the processes, we are training and retraining every worker in the statistical process-control methods. Etc, etc, etc.

If this list is just a list of excuses, and not the real thing, we are facing two huge problems, not just one. The first is that we are using lack of information as an excuse, and thus maybe the reason for not having enough information stems simply from not defining it correctly. The second problem is the diverse approach the company has taken to make improvements. It might be erroneous. How can we test it?

Maybe the best way is to once again conduct a *Gedunken* experiment. Let's suppose that our current efforts to improve are successful beyond our wildest dreams. Let's suppose that we tackled each item on the list and had spectacular success. None of the problems listed above still exists in our plant. We now have what some would call a perfect plant. Everything is fixed, every piece of data is precisely known. Do we have the information? Do we know precisely how much net profit our company will make next quarter?

Let's describe our perfect plant. Let's give all the data that somebody might think is required. In our plant, we have rationalized our product portfolio so that we have only two products; let's call them P and Q. These are very good products, and our work force is very well trained to produce them; the defect rate is zero—not one PPM—zero.

Now, the selling price. The selling price of these two products is fixed to the cent. We have overcome the syndrome of every salesman offering deals to different clients. They are disciplined by now. Can you imagine such a world? Selling price for P is, let's say, $90 per unit, and for Q, a little bit more, $100 per unit.

What about the sales forecast? Here, a big surprise is waiting. The forecast is no longer a guesstimate. It is precise to the single piece. I call the forecast "market potential." The market potential for P is 100 units per week, and for Q, only 50 units per week. Let's clarify what is meant by market potential. It is not what we have committed to deliver. We are so good, we do not have to commit to anything. These numbers represent what the market will buy from us, if we just deliver. Of course, P having a market potential of 100 units per week means that if we produce more than 100 units per week, we are stuck with finished goods.

Now, let's look at the engineering data. Product P is made by assembling one part that we purchase, and two parts that we manufacture in-house. Each of the parts that we manufacture is processed from purchased material through two distinct processes (see Figure 1).

Note that the same structure could describe different envi-

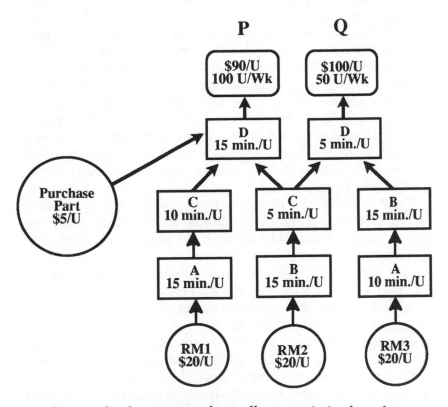

1 Our artificial company where all uncertainties have been removed.

ronments, such as a layout of product design, a project, or even a decision process—it all looks the same. We have to stick to one specific terminology, otherwise nothing will be clearly understood, but this does not mean that we are necessarily dealing only with a production environment. What we are actually trying to describe here is the generic case of "using resources to fulfill tasks in order to achieve a predetermined objective." Now we have to have some numerical data. This will certainly force us into more specific terminology; nevertheless, let's not forget that this is an example of a far more generic situation.

Let's assume the price we pay for the purchased part is $5 per unit, while the price we pay for the raw material is, in each case, $20 per unit. The first material starts its "journey" through department A. It could be engineer-type A, or warehouse location A, or salesman in region A, or manager level A. . . . In this experiment we are talking about a production environment, so let's use the terminology of a worker with skill A. And let's assume that it takes this worker fifteen minutes to process one unit. Of course, if we were in a process environment, we would use pieces per hour, or in engineering we would use days or weeks (and pray that it wouldn't take years). The environment dictates the terminology. Here we are using terminology of minutes per unit.

The first process of the second material is done by another type of worker, a worker with skill B, and it takes exactly the same amount of time—15 minutes per unit. The second processing stage of both parts is done by a third type of worker, a worker with skill C. It takes him 10 minutes per unit to do the first part, but only 5 minutes per unit for the second part. This of course implies that the worker performing skill C is not dedicated to the production of just one type of part, but is a multi-purpose worker. Do you have multi-purpose resources? Not sure? Do you have set-up? If the answer is yes, you have multi-purpose resources. In our case, the set-up is zero. We are so good that we have reduced all set-up to zero—not to one second, but actually zero.

Assembly is done by assembly worker D. It takes him 15

minutes to assemble one unit. This completes the data for product P. Now, let's describe product Q.

Product Q is assembled from only two parts. Since we have embarked on group technology we are trying to use as few designs as possible, so Q will be assembled from the second part of P, and another part that is processed in our plant, in two distinct steps (see Figure 1). This of course will make the middle part a common part for two different products, a very ordinary case in industry. Nevertheless, let's clarify it. In order to deliver one P and one Q, two units of the middle part are necessary. Why do we stress it? Because, for example, in design engineering, the same figure will imply that we need to design the middle part only once, even though it is required for the design of both P and Q. The environment dictates even the interpretation of the flow diagram.

Now let's complete the data. The raw material of the third part is purchased for the same price as the other two, $20 per unit. Its first stage of processing is done, let's say, by the same worker A who does the first part. (We have launched in our plant an extensive cross-training "Job enrichment program.") It takes 10 minutes to process one unit of the third part. The second process is done by worker B, the same worker B who did the first stage on the second part, and it takes him the same amount of time—15 minutes per unit. The assembly is done by the same assembly worker D, but in this case it only takes 5 minutes to assemble one unit.

In our plant, there are four different skills of workers, A, B, C, and D. Even though we have done extensive cross training, we still have four different types of resources. I do not believe that we will ever reach the point where everybody will be able to do everything. Where can we find the genius who will persuade a lathe to do welding also? But even if we can do that, we certainly can not find anyone who will be able to persuade the chief engineer to sweep the floor in another department. So even in our ideal plant, we still have distinct skills. Everyone who could have been trained to do additional work has been cross-trained already. Let's not fall into the trap of using one skill to do all jobs.

Now the question is, "How many workers with each skill do we have?" This time we will be really merciful. We will not say that we have 17 skill-A workers on the first shift, but only 12 on the second, but on Saturday, worker B can, if compensated by an additional 27.945 percent, do the job of . . . No, we will be merciful. Let's take the simplest possible case. In our plant, we have only one A, one B, one C, and one D, and they are totally non-interchangeable. B cannot do the work of A, and A cannot do the work of B.

For how long is each one of these resources available in the plant? Let's again take the simplest case. Let's assume that each one of the workers is available for 5 days a week, 8 hours a day, 60 minutes an hour. This is 2400 minutes per week. Have you noticed, no absenteeism? They are not even going to the toilet.

What else is missing? The operating expense. Let's assume that the total operating expense of the plant is $6000 per week. Maybe some reminders will be useful. What do we call operating expense? This $6000 includes the salaries of these workers, their fringe benefits, the salaries of the foremen, the company's sales people, management, and the money that we pay to the utilities for energy and to the banks for interest. All of it is included in the $6000. But what is not included?

Let's repeat it. What is not included is the money that we pay to our vendors for materials and purchased parts. This money is not operating expense, it is inventory. If we want to sell anything we will have to buy material. How much will we have to pay? That depends on the quantities that we buy. The price per unit is already given for each material. But remember, this money is in addition to the $6000.

Everything is given. Everything is precise. No excuses. So let's repeat the original question. Not exactly—since everything is specified per week, let's rephrase it in the following way: "What is the maximum net profit (minimum loss) this company is capable of earning per week?" We have all the data, it is available and accurate. Do we have the information? Can we answer the managerial question?

I strongly recommend that you take the time now to try and solve this quiz on your own, before continuing to read. It will shed a whole new light on what we intuitively call information; it is quite different from the common use of this word.

13. *Demonstrating the difference between the Cost World and the Throughput World*

During the last two years I have had the opportunity to present the quiz suggested above to over 10,000 managers. It is amazing, but on the average, only one out of a hundred have succeeded in solving it correctly. This is not the most interesting fact. What is much more important is the way most managers usually address the question.

Most of them are very systematic. They start with the question, and remembering the definition of net profit (throughput minus operating expense), they immediately embark on calculating the missing piece, throughput. Let's follow their footsteps.

Throughput is achieved through sale of the products. Let's start with product P. How much can be sold per week? One hundred units. For each of them, the clients are willing to pay $90. But if we just multiply these two numbers we'll get sales, not throughput. In order to calculate the throughput, we have to subtract from the selling price the amount we have to pay to the vendors. In the case of product P, it is $45. Thus the throughput generated through product P is:

$$P: 100 \text{ units} \times (\$90 - \$45) = \$4500$$

Now let's do the same for Q. The amount that can be sold per week is 50 units. Each unit brings $100, but each unit necessitates a payment to the vendors of $40. The throughput achieved through product Q is:

$$Q: 50 \text{ units} \times (\$100 - \$40) = \$3000$$

The total throughput of the company is the summation of the throughput of the individual products; it comes to $7500. But this is not net profit. To arrive at net profit, we have to subtract the $6000 of operating expense (we've already taken care of the money paid to the vendors). The net profit per week will be:

$$NP = \$7500 - \$6000 = \$1500$$

Very straightforward. Very wrong. It is amazing to what extent this answer is overwhelmingly the most common answer. People do not obey their intuition, but their training. What should always be the first step in approaching any system? We have agreed on it before; IDENTIFY THE SYSTEM'S CONSTRAINT(S). Before doing that, any calculation will be just an empty exercise.

In the above calculation we have assumed that the market is the only constraint. Why? Maybe there is an internal constraint? In this case there definitely is; very likely you have identified it already. Nevertheless, let's do the steps systematically (systematically does not necessarily mean correctly). For this case we are going to use the numbers—the data—in order to identify the constraints. In real life, we have to realize that the data is usually rotten.

Every MRP expert knows that if the time to process a part has to be checked, it is better to ask the foreman, not the engineer. The foreman will most likely cheat you, about 30 percent, but you know exactly in which direction he is cheating. The engineer might mislead you by 200 percent, and you don't even know in which direction! Any information system worth anything will have to identify the very few pieces of data from which the information was derived. This data must be carefully verified. Otherwise, we will have to check the validity of all data elements. This is an impossibility, as thousands of companies have found out; so much time and effort was "invested" in the last twenty years to arrive at this realization. Let's not waste this knowledge.

But in this experiment, we stated that the data is perfectly accurate, so we can proceed. What we want to do is to find out if there is an internal physical constraint. There might be another type of constraint, policy constraints, but they cannot be found through the data. To find them directly, we need the scientific method of problem identification—the effect-cause-effect technique. Policy constraints are outside the scope of information systems, and thus, every information system must make the daring assumption of "no policy constraints."

To identify internal resource constraints, we simply have to calculate the load placed by the forecast on each resource, and compare it to the resource's availability. For resource A, the load placed by product P per week is 100 units times 15 minutes per unit, or 1500 minutes. Product Q places an additional load on resource A of 50 units times 10 minutes, bringing the load to a grand total of 2000 minutes per week. The availability of resource A is 2400 minutes per week. No problem here.

Resource B: Product P places a load per week of 100 units times 15 minutes per unit, or 1500 minutes. Product Q places a load of 50 units times 30 minutes. Yes, only 30 minutes, even though it is processed through two different jobs; we have stated that set-up is zero. The grand total in this case is 3000 minutes per week, far exceeding the availability. We definitely have a resource constraint.

Doing the same calculations for resources C and D shows in each case that the load is only 1750 minutes per week. No problem whatsoever. B is the only resource constraint, and it stands out like a sore thumb, exactly as in reality whenever a real bottleneck exists.

Now, we are facing a decision. It is obvious that we cannot satisfy the entire market potential—we don't have enough capacity from resource B. So we have to choose which products, and in what quantities, we are going to offer the market. Most managers that have reached this point in the experiment (they did not fall into the first trap), proceed in the following way: We cannot satisfy the entire market, so let's offer the market the most profitable product that we have, the star. If we still have residual capacity, we will offer the dog. Makes sense.

Okay, what is the most profitable product? Let's examine it from more than one angle. First let's look at the selling price. P is sold for $90 per unit, and Q is sold for $100 per unit. If this was the only consideration, which product would you like to sell? Certainly Q.

Now let's examine through the eyes of the material. P requires that we pay our vendors $45 per unit; Q requires only $40 per unit. So if that was the only concern, which product would you prefer to sell? Again the same answer, Q.

We can also look on throughput, which is selling price minus raw material price. It leads to the same place. The throughput for P is $45, while for Q, $60.

But these are not the only concerns. We also usually look at the amount of effort needed to produce a product for the market. Calculating the amount of effort for product P, we reach the number:

$$15 + 15 + 10 + 5 + 15 = 60 \text{ minutes of effort.}$$

As for product Q, the same calculation leads us to:

$$15 + 10 + 5 + 15 + 5 = 50 \text{ minutes of effort.}$$

From the point of view of effort, which product would you prefer to sell? Once again, the same product, Q. It is very important to realize that since all three concerns have led, in our case, to the same conclusion, it indicates that any cost system in the world, no matter what overhead factors we used, would give the same answer: Q is definitely a more profitable product than P.

Okay, using this as a guideline, let's now calculate the net profit. The first product to offer the market is Q. We can sell 50 units of Q per week. These 50 units each demand 30 minutes on our constraint (resource B), absorbing 1500 minutes of its available time per week. This leaves only 900 minutes to be used for the production of P. How many P's can we produce in 900 minutes? Each P requires 15 minutes from resource B, so we will be able to produce and offer the market only 60 units of P per week. Yes, the market wants 100 units per week, but what can we do? We do not have enough capacity.

The best mix that we can offer the market is 50 Q's and 60 P's per week. Product Q will bring 50 units × $60 = $3000 throughput dollars, and product P will bring 60 units × $45 = $2700 throughput dollars. The total throughput will be $5,700 per week, minus operating expense, which is $6000 . . . Whoops! We are going to lose $300 per week. Oh well, what can we do? The Japanese have entered our markets and. . . .

Try to imagine what happens to a manager who promises corporate $1500 plus per week, and delivers a $300 loss! How long will this situation last before he will be forced to pay a visit to his friendly neighborhood headhunter? We can ignore our constraints; they will never ignore us.

But wait, this last calculation is not in line with the "throughput world." Using the terminology of constraints is not enough. We must get rid of the mental blocks planted by the "cost world." This last calculation, as you have no doubt noticed, uses the wrong terminology of "product profit." In the throughput world there is no such thing as product profit, there is only company's profit.

Let's try again. How should we go about calculating net profit? We have outlined the process to be used for any managerial question. What is the second focusing step? DECIDE HOW TO EXPLOIT THE CONSTRAINT. What have we tried to exploit? Labor efforts. Why? Is it because we don't have enough of A, or C, or D? No. So why do we do the calculation described above? Because we do not have enough of resource B.

What does it mean to exploit the constraint? It does not

mean "Make it work all the time." Remember, the goal of the company is not to make the employees work, it is to make more money now as well as in the future. What we want is to get the maximum money for the things that limit us, for the constraint. When we offer the market product P, the market pays $45 for the company's efforts. Remember, $45 of the $90 selling price is paid for the efforts of the vendors. But how many minutes of the constraint do we have to invest in order to get these 45 throughput dollars? B has to invest 15 minutes. So when we offer product P to the market, we get three throughput dollars ($45/15:00) per minute of our constraint.

When we offer Q to the market the company gets $60 throughput dollars, but we have to invest 30 minutes of the constraint. Thus, when Q is offered to the market, we receive only $2 per minute ($60/30:00) of our constraint. Notice, these two and three dollars per minute do not have anything to do with cost, they are throughput contributions. With these numbers in front of us, and being convinced of the need to exploit the constraint, now what do we prefer to sell? The exact opposite of the answer of all the cost systems in the world.

Who is right? All the cost systems, or our common-sense intuition? There is only one judge, the bottom line. So let's calculate what will be the end result if we will elect to follow our intuition. Let's offer P to the market first. How many P's can we possibly sell per week? 100 units. How many minutes of the constraint are required? Fifteen hundred minutes. Only 900 minutes are now left for Q. Each Q requires 30 minutes on the constraint. Thus, only 30 Q's will be offered to the market. The mix is now 100 P's and 30 Q's per week.

Wait a minute. Do we understand the meaning of this last statement? Show me a manager who will stand up and say, "Yes, we have a star and a dog. Let's ignore the star and push the dog as much as we can, and only if we have residual capacity will we graciously offer the star as well." What do you think about this manager's chances of being promoted? Thank God that we are dealing here with just a quiz, so let's proceed.

Product P will bring $100 \times 45 = \$4500$ throughput dollars per week, while Q will add to it another $30 \times 60 = 1800$ throughput dollars per week. The total throughput of the company will now be $6300. Subtracting $6000 for operating expense per week, the net profit of the same company is now plus $300 per week. Plus or minus, who cares?

Who is affected by what we have just done? Shareholders, top management, and finance—no doubt. But who else? Production people? Not at all. It is our sales force. Think about it. Currently, for which product would we pay a higher commission? Product Q—it is the more "profitable" product. If Q carries a higher commission than P, which product will our sales people push into the market? Once they have sold Q, we might know that it is preferable to sell P, but now it's too late. We must deliver what they sold.

Production doesn't really care if they have to produce more of this or that part. Anyway, worker B is working at full speed. What the last calculation indicates is that in trying to make more money, we need to initiate a drastic change in our sales commission schemes. This is the meaning of dependency; we may deal with, let's say, production, but the conclusions may impact mainly another department, this time the sales force.

A small example of the difference between the "cost world" and thinking according to the reality of "throughput world." But now let's go back and do what we originally intended to do, evaluate the ramifications on our information problem.

14. *Clarifying the confusion between data and information—some fundamental definitions*

What was the actual information we wanted? The amount of net profit we are going to make. To get the answer we needed first of all to make a decision, "Which product mix should we offer to the market?" This decision, in turn, was based on the identification of the company's constraints—only this last step depends on what we used to call data; things like time to process a unit, resource availability, and sales forecast. A "chain" is starting to emerge, a chain in which each link might be considered as both data and information, depending on the side from which we look at it.

To clarify the last statement, let's ask ourselves, once again, the key question of our discussion: "What is data and what is information?" What did we say right at the start of our discussion? "The content of a warehouse is data, but for the person who has to respond to an urgent client demand, it is information." We already had the impression that the same string of characters could be data or information. Now, I think, we have a little deeper understanding. The relation DATA/INFORMATION is even more intriguing than it originally appeared.

Let's examine it more carefully. "Resource B is a constraint." Is this data or information? For the production manager, it is certainly information. It answers his major question, "On which resource should we concentrate?" But at the same time, for the sales manager it is just data; the sales manager's question is "Which product should we push into the market?" The desired product mix, "Push P and only then Q," is clearly information for the sales manager. Can it be derived without knowing that B is a constraint? No. "B is a constraint" is thus a link that for one manager is information, and at the same time, for another manager, it is a piece of required data.

But that is not the only link in our chain. For example, the top manager's question was "How much net profit are we going to make?" The answer to this question—"$300"—is information, while the statement "It is preferable to sell P rather than Q," is not information, but data.

It seems that information is not the data required to answer the question, but it is the answer itself. Data seems to be the "pieces" that are needed in order to answer this question. What about our previous definition—any string of characters that describes anything about our reality? It looks as if we have to distinguish further between "data" and "required data." Wait, this is important. Making a mistake at the level of the basic definitions may lead the entire discussion to a confusing chaos. We should reexamine our definitions in less complicated situations, in daily life situations, where our intuition is the strongest. We must check to see if these proposed formal definitions of information and data really match our intuitive sense of these words.

Let's take a case where you ask your secretary a question like "What is the best way to reach Atlanta today?" I would expect an answer such as "You should catch this flight." Such an answer we would, no doubt, call information. Of course, if this particular flight does not go to Atlanta, I would still call it information, it is simply erroneous information. However, if instead of a straightforward answer, I am handed the entire flight catalog, I would be less pleased. Instead of information I received data. For the secretary, the same flight catalog is information. His/her question is "What are all the possible flights to

Atlanta?" Even in this simple case we see that what is regarded as data and what is regarded as information depend on the question asked; what is considered at one level to be information, might be just data at another level.

What words will we use if an outdated flight catalog was handed to us? It is still data. We can not even call it erroneous data. Remember, data is any string of characters that describes something about our reality. It seems that an additional term of "required data" would be very useful. Yes, now the above definitions feel much more in line with our intuitive understanding.

Now, I think, we are in a better position to realize the validity of what we said right at the beginning of our discussion: "What is data and what is information is in the eyes of the beholder." Did we need to spend all this time to analyze the "new philosophy" just to gain a little deeper understanding? I believe the answer is definitely yes. Defining information as "The answer to the question asked" means that information can be deduced only as a result of using a decision process. Required data is an input to the decision process, information is an output, the decision process itself must be embedded in an information system. No, we certainly haven't wasted our time in trying to formalize the new decision process.

There is a key word hiding in what we said just now; let's not miss it. We came to the conclusion that information is arranged in a hierarchical way, that at each level the information is DEDUCED from the data. The word DEDUCE is a key word. It reveals that in order to derive information, we need something else besides data; we must have the deduction process, or as have we have referred to it up to now, the decision process.

What was illustrated so clearly by the above quiz? All the data elements we needed were available. Nevertheless, we were unable to deduce the desired information—the net profit. Even worse, we have been misled to deduce an erroneous answer.

Two conditions must be met in order to acquire information. Data is certainly one of the conditions, but the decision procedure itself is no less important. Without the proper decision process there is no way to deduce the needed information from the data. In the past, we were immersed in the "cost world"; the decision process was totally inadequate, and that's why we were unable to get the desired information.

Our frustration has led us to intensify our efforts, but they were channelled in the wrong direction. Rather than seeking the appropriate decision process, we simply expended our effort to assemble more data and then, when this didn't help, more accurate data. The detailed decision procedures, and thus the generic decision process, must be an integral part of an information system.

The FIVE FOCUSING STEPS seem to give us the needed generic decision process that enables us to climb the information ladder: from basic data to the next level, that of identifying the systems constraints, then to the higher level of deducing tactical answers, which finally leads to the financial bottom line information.

I hear what you say: one tiny example, and without any hesitation, this funny person jumps to world-encompassing conclusions. But wait—these conclusions were not derived from the example, they stem directly from the FIVE FOCUSING STEPS of your common-sense intuition. The example was just an illustration. Never mind, we'll have many more examples to discuss anyhow.

What we should bear in mind is that the five steps by themselves are not sufficient. To actually climb the information ladder we have to develop the detailed procedures that stem from them. For example, the way that we used the second step—the EXPLOIT concept—was not exactly trivial. The procedure of determining the proper product mix according to "throughput dollars per constraint unit" is very simple, but not easy to find. Moreover, you and I know that the procedure we used does not cover the general case. The quest to determine the proper product mix is not yet ended.

Before we continue to explore the ramifications of the FIVE FOCUSING STEPS on other tactical issues, before we further examine the scope of the resulting decision procedures, maybe we should devote some time to the data issue. You see, it has been so long that we have been desperately trying to get the needed information by expanding our efforts to collect data, that maybe we have gone overboard in that direction. It might be that we are exaggerating in our perception of how much data is really needed and how much effort actually should be devoted to increase its accuracy.

Just review what we have done in the quiz. We needed data, but not all the data. Ask yourself, did we need to know the "cost per hour" of each one of the resources? Today we spend so much time and effort to pin it down; for what purpose? To control our expenses we need to know how much money we pay to each category, how many dollars for salary and fringes we pay the workers, but the "cost per hour?" This is an intermediate link that was assumed to be necessary under the COST decision process. This step turns out to be totally redundant under the new decision process. How many more such anachronisms exist? We will have to be very alert to weed them all out.

Let's go over, once again, these most important conclusions.

Take a deep breath and dive into this long chain of logical connections; what did we say? Since information is built in a hierarchical structure and since the decision process itself is the ingredient that enables us to climb from one information level to the other, it implies that any change in the decision process might make obsolete an entire level of "information." Something that was considered as a data/information link, something that had to be deduced from the data in order to enable the derivation of a higher level of information, might be totally unneeded when the mode of deduction is changed.

We already started to suspect that this is actually the case, when we examined the need for "cost per hour," but it might be worthwhile to explore if there are more such examples, or is this just an isolated case?

One of the most sought after types of data is "product cost." Sometimes controllers and MIS managers break their hearts trying to get a good handle on it. Why do we need this piece of data; in order to determine the selling price? This cannot be the reason; the price of a product is not determined by us, it is determined by our markets. To find out how to price the product we must look outside. Looking inside, into our own operation, will not lead us anywhere.

Why do we need the "product cost"? In order to make decisions, like determining which product we should push into the market and which product we should refrain from pushing. Yes, this is the only reason; but let's face it, the quiz vividly showed that this decision cannot possibly be made using the notion of "product cost." All cost systems would have indicated that Q should be pushed into the market—our bottom line showed just the opposite. "Product cost," as we indicated earlier, is a concept which must be eliminated, along with its creator, the decision process based on the "cost world."

What about data accuracy? Does it really behoove us to know every piece of data to its ultimate accuracy? Just ask yourself, out of all the process times appearing in our quiz, which one needed to be accurate? To identify the constraint we didn't need high accuracy at all. If resource D is going to be loaded for 1000 minutes per week or for 2000 minutes per week, who really cares? We needed to be accurate only to the level sufficient to know if a resource is or isn't a constraint.

The process times on resource B needed to be much more accurate. We used them as data for a higher level of information —to determine the desired product mix. But even here there is no need to go overboard—we still don't need very high accuracy. If the process times were 17 minutes rather then 15, we would nevertheless arrive at the same conclusion. Only when we are dealing with the highest information level, "What will be the net profit?"—only then do these two process times need to be accurate; their accuracy will determine the accuracy of the derived information. All other process times could have large inaccuracies without affecting the end result at all.

This is something that we'll have to get used to. In the cost world we were under the impression that increasing the accuracy of any required data would increase the accuracy of the end result; thus striving for better accuracy was a way of life. This is no longer the case. In the throughput world, most required data has a boundary, and increasing accuracy beyond this boundary does not have any impact at all on the end results. Very often, better data accuracy is not translated into better information.

Managers need data in order to enable them to make decisions, in order to derive the needed information. A change in the decision process implies not just a change in the end result, in the information, but also implies a change in the nature of the required data and in its needed level of accuracy. What we have seen in the previous chapter was an example of such change.

This chapter has been more than a little bit crowded. Maybe an intermediate summary would be helpful—if not a summary then at least a list of definitions of the terms that we have spread so generously throughout the last pages.

INFORMATION: An answer to the question asked.

ERRONEOUS INFORMATION: A wrong answer to the question asked.

DATA: Any string of characters that describes something about our reality.

REQUIRED DATA: The data needed by the decision procedure to derive the information.

ERRONEOUS DATA: A string of characters that does not describe reality (might be a residual of an erroneous decision procedure).

INVALID DATA: Data that is not needed to deduce the specific desired information.

Let's leave the data issue for now and continue to explore the ramifications of the decision process on other aspects of our company, using the same exact quiz.

15. *Demonstrating the impact of the new decision process on some tactical issues*

It might be a good idea to first get a somewhat better appreciation of the ramifications of switching to a new decision process. This might shed some new light on the quality of the attainable information, as well as give us some preliminary feeling as to the required data and its level of desired accuracy. So, let's use the same quiz in order to highlight the change in a totally different aspect of our company.

Suppose that I am the foreman in charge of work center A. You are the plant manager. I come to you and ask, "How many items of each part should I process per week?" Since the goal of the plant is to make more money, your answer will probably be: "Produce 100 P's and 30 Q's." Makes sense, but you have just put me in a very unpleasant situation. I have to remind you, with all due respect, that I probably don't understand your answer. Being a foreman in the area that produces parts, my terminology is "part number," not products. Realizing that, you switch to the terminology of the person who must execute the instruction.

From the left-hand part, you will ask me to produce 100 items per week, from the middle part, nothing (being the foreman of work center A, I do not have anything to do with the middle part) and from the right hand part, just 30 items. What you have done is simply to follow, intuitively, the third step—

86

SUBORDINATE EVERYTHING ELSE TO THE ABOVE DECISION.

But now see what will happen to me. Remember that I am still the foreman of work center A. How much time do I have to invest in order to produce 100 items of the left-hand part? Each of them requires 15 minutes; thus, the time required is 1500 minutes. Nothing is required for the middle part, and 30 times 10 minutes for the right-hand part.

If I produce more, do I help the company? Definitely not. The excess parts will not be turned into throughput; B's capacity is the one that determines the throughput. Any additional production will just inflate the inventory. But how much total time do I need to fully produce your requirements? $1500 + 300 = 1800$ minutes. How much time is available for my work center? Twenty-four hundred minutes. So if I do exactly what you have asked me to do, what will happen to my "efficiencies"? They will drop. What will happen to my head? It will probably drop too.

If I do exactly what you want me to do I am going to be punished. So what do you think I will actually do? I'll talk with my friends, the scheduler or the warehouse manager—if needed, I will even steal material. I am going to make my numbers. And remember, the corpse is not going to be found in my department, the inventory will accumulate downstream, in finished parts, in finished goods. In no-man's-land.

What choice do you give me? Do what is right and be punished, or play the numbers game and be a hero. What do you think I am—a saint, or even worse, a martyr?

The realization of the "throughput world" that mandates the third focusing step, "Subordinate everything else to the above decision," implies a drastic change in our local performance measurements. How long can we continue to reward stupidity and punish the right actions? How much money, time, and effort is devoted today to gather data for local performance measurements, just so that the end result will distort the behavior of the people we are measuring?

Today if you say: "Produce only a hundred of these and then

thirty of those and then stop," what do you think will register in the minds of the workers? When was the last time that management told them to stop working? It was five minutes before the layoffs! Every one of the workers will instinctively slow down to prove that you need them. The subject that we have just touched on is very sensitive; changing the local performance measurements borders on changing the "work ethic."

What is the current "work ethic"? I think that we can summarize it in one phrase:

"IF A WORKER DOES NOT HAVE ANYTHING TO DO, FIND HIM SOMETHING TO DO!"

The SUBORDINATION concept is in direct contradiction with current behavior. Let's not fool ourselves that changing the local performance measurements will be an easy task. Yes, we can, without too much hassle, devise the procedures to get the vital information of what each one is supposed to do. As a matter of fact, we will find that we need to assemble significantly less data, and the requirements for its accuracy will be reduced. But this is not the real issue. Do you really believe that we can change the culture through changing the local performance measurements? It is not that simple. Previously, we said, "Tell me how you measure me and I will tell you how I will behave," but now, let's remind ourselves of the other half of the story: CHANGE MY MEASUREMENTS TO NEW ONES, THAT I DON'T FULLY COMPREHEND, AND NOBODY KNOWS HOW I WILL BEHAVE, NOT EVEN ME.

We cannot change a culture by simply changing the performance measurements.

The transformation from the "cost world" to the "throughput world"—the new decision process—allows us, for the first time, to construct a relatively simple information system—but its usage is totally dependent on the ability of the company to transform its culture.

At this stage, let's just make a note that we need to develop the new local performance measurements, certainly a necessary piece of the needed information system. But for now, let's continue to explore more ramifications of the change, so that the entire picture will continue to unfold.

Suppose we have already developed all the needed tools for the new work ethic. Companies that have already made the switch have found that, contrary to common belief, workers look for work. Some companies have even gone to the extent of putting newspaper stands on the floor; this didn't help. The idle time that is an unavoidable result of forcing non-constraint resources to refrain from overproducing must be filled with something meaningful.

To use the free time to improve local processes seems a natural solution. Unfortunately, our workers are usually much more "innocent" than we are—they are not as good at deceiving themselves. Giving them meaningless "improvement programs," which do not lead to actual improvement in the performance of the company, cannot be the answer for the long run.

We must devise the procedure that will give us, on an ongoing basis, the ability to identify the most needed local improvement actions. This is not exactly a new need, but in the "throughput world" setting, this information becomes almost mandatory. So, let's explore the subject of "process improvement," but in order to make the discussion more vivid, let's approach it in the following way. . . .

Let's suppose that now I am a process engineer. I was a foreman, but I went to night school, got my degree, and you have promoted me to be a process engineer. I am no longer a foreman, I was promoted. You have not been promoted. You are still the plant manager.

Suppose that, tomorrow, I enter your office—you have an open-door policy—and I tell you the following: "There is one part in our plant that we produce in large quantities; it is one of the more important parts. For each unit, we have to invest twenty minutes of process time—yes, twenty minutes. I have an idea. Just authorize $2000 for a fixture. . . . OK, maybe a little bit more, but certainly $3000 will be sufficient. Once we have this fixture, I can show you that we can produce the part, not in twenty minutes but in . . . twenty-one minutes."

What will be your reaction? Am I back to being foreman? If I'm lucky! Suppose that you have infinite patience, and you inquire to see if maybe quality will be improved by this change. "No," is my answer. Will less material be required? "No, no change there." Well?

What was my only mistake? I took management's direction too seriously. They told me to ELEVATE THE SYSTEM'S CONSTRAINTS; they even told me that resource B is the constraint. "Do something about it, every drop counts. Every minute saved on the constraint is important." When I asked what to do about all the projects that I'm already involved in, they dismissed them out-of-hand. "They are all revolving around improving non-constraints; just forget them." That is what they said. I love my job; I enjoy working for my company. So I went home and racked my brain, to figure out how to elevate the constraint. I found a way. Now I am fired.

You see, the initial puzzled reaction to my suggestion was a "cost world" reaction. In the "cost world" there is no way that increasing the total time to produce an item will be beneficial. But in the "throughput world"? My idea was the following:

With the new fixture we can reduce the time the constraint takes to produce the middle part. This fixture will enable us to off-load some of the work from resource B to resource C. Now it will take only fourteen minutes, rather than fifteen, to produce the middle part on the constraint. We can off-load one minute to resource C, but C is slower than B, so now the middle part will require on C, not five minutes, but seven. The end result is that the total time to process the middle part will go from twenty minutes to 21 minutes. Exactly as I said.

If my suggestion were taken seriously, how many weeks would it have taken to recover the $3000 investment in the fixture? Of course, in the "cost world," never. In the JIT or TQM world, investments are justified by just labeling them "improvements." But we have to answer in the actual world, in the world where the goal of the company is not to reduce cost or to "improve" but to make more money.

Because of this fixture, we can free up one minute per unit from the constraint. We are producing 130 units per week of the middle part, which means that we will have an additional 130 constraint minutes per week on our hands. What can we sell one minute of the constraint for? We calculated it before—no, the answer is not $3 per minute, since we have already satisfied all of the market potential for P, but we still have unsatisfied market for Q. We still can sell additional minutes of the constraint for $2 per minute. This means that buying the fixture will contribute $130 \times 2 = 260$ throughput dollars per week. Since the operating expenses stay the same, this change in throughput will nicely glide down to the bottom line. To cover $3000, we will need a little bit less than 12 weeks. Quite a good investment, isn't it?

Under the "cost world" mentality, no engineer will dare to suggest such a "disprovement," raising the process time from 20 to 21 minutes. A foreman in charge of both work centers B and C might do such a thing, but then he will be very careful to disguise it. If reported precisely, the foreman will be punished, because he increased his variances. He has invested more in the part than the standards call for.

What data do our process engineers need? They need to know which resources are constraints, and for how much can we sell each additional minute that we can squeeze out of them. That's all. What data do we supply to the process engineers instead? Oceans of what we call "cost" information. What is the result? Another engineer will come knocking on your door with the following suggestion: "We can improve the second operation of the left-hand part. For an investment of $3000 in some tools, we will be able to reduce the process time from ten minutes to just five." And we will probably give him the "engineer of the year" award. What did we get in return?

No, the answer is not zero. Negative impact exists as well, and I do not mean just a $3000 investment down the drain. We now have something much much worse; we now have a very proud engineer—proud for the wrong reasons. We have misled a very scarce and expensive person to focus his attention, now as well as in the future, in the wrong places.

How many companies do you know of that have "cost reduction programs"? If all these cost reductions actually materialized on the bottom line, these companies would have been extremely profitable. Where do cost reductions disappear? Now we know the answer; they were not cost reductions to start with. How can we have cost reductions if operating expenses are not cut? They are just number games. When operating expenses are basically fixed, the only way to increase net profit is by increasing throughput.

What is information? What data do we need in order to deduce it? How accurate should this data be? These questions start to have a new meaning. Maybe, after all, we haven't wasted our time discussing the NEW OVERALL MANAGEMENT PHILOSOPHY.

16. *Demonstrating inertia as a cause for policy constraints*

Since we are immersed in the quiz and know it now by heart, why don't we continue to use it. Remember, we still have not yet explored the power of the fifth focusing step.

Suppose that our director of marketing has seen what we have done, and realizing the validity of the fourth step—ELEVATE THE SYSTEM'S CONSTRAINTS—jumps on the band wagon. He rightfully claims that there is another constraint in our company, in addition to resource B; part of the market potential is also a constraint.

No, stating that the market POTENTIAL is a constraint is wrong; it might drive our sales force to get more orders for Q. That will certainly not help our bottom line. What is a constraint? Alleviate the restriction and you will make more money. If we alleviate the restriction without impacting the bottom line, it is a very clear indication we are not dealing with a constraint.

The constraint here is insufficient market demand for product P; if we get more market potential for product P, we can make more money. Our marketing director highlights the fact that our company does not sell anything to, let's say, Japan. His suggestion is that he should go to Japan to find out if there is a market for our products.

Two weeks later he returns and proudly presents his findings. Let's accept his findings as part of the quiz—not just for the current question, but for all future questions as well. What he tells us is the following: "There is a beautiful market in Japan for our products. They are waiting to buy P's, they are waiting to buy Q's. They love them! Moreover, the market over there is big. In fact, it is as big as our domestic market; we can sell up to 50 Q's a week and/or up to 100 P's a week. But there is a small tiny problem. . . ."

Somehow, whenever we talk to marketing people, at the end, there is always a tiny problem. Yes, your guess is correct. If we want to sell in Japan, we will have to discount our selling price by 20 percent. But, marketing guarantees that this price reduction will not impact our domestic prices. He checked thoroughly. We can give reduced prices in Japan without affecting prices here. They want a slight change in our product that will allow for this price differentiation, a change that will not require any real additional efforts.

Do I hear the word *dumping?* What is not allowed in dumping? To sell below cost? If product cost does not exist, how can we sell below it? And besides, where do you prefer to buy a Japanese camera, in Manhattan or in Tokyo? In Manhattan, right? Why? Because it is cheaper there. Why is it cheaper in Manhattan? Ah, everybody knows, transportation prices are negative.

We wouldn't think of going to Japan to sell Q for 20 percent less. We don't sell all our Q's here for $100, why go all the way to Japan just to sell them for $80? But should we or shouldn't we go to Japan to sell P for . . . $72?

A very, very difficult question in the "cost world." A very easy one in the "throughput world." We have a situation where operating expenses are fixed, and the resource constraint cannot yet be elevated. What is the only way to increase net profit? To improve the exploitation of the constraint. Right now, the minimum that we get for the constraint is $2 per minute. If we can get more than $2 per minute in Japan, we should sell there. It will definitely increase our bottom line. Otherwise, the only reason to go to Japan would be just for a sightseeing trip.

The selling price in Japan is $72. From that we have to subtract the raw materials, which are $45. Somehow, our vendors charge the same, without considering where we sell the final product. No patriotism. The throughput per unit is thus $27. We still have to invest into it 15 minutes of the constraint, making the ratio of throughput dollars per constraint minute less than two. Under this scenario, we should not go to Japan.

What is the data our sales people need (assuming, of course, perfect market segmentation)? The dollar-value of the raw-material in each product; the number of constraint minutes for each product; and one additional number, the threshold level— the minimum that we are getting today per constraint minute. How should they determine the required information? At what price to sell, if at all? Under perfect segmentation they should charge whatever the market will bear. If the market price puts us below this threshold, they should not accept the order. Pretty simple, isn't it? What "information" do we give them instead? Let's not even think about it.

But now, let's be a little bit more serious. This quiz does not represent a real-life plant. What is the situation described in the quiz? The clients are banging on our doors, wanting to buy our products, holding the checks in their hands, and just because of one lousy machine, we cannot accept their checks? What would we usually do in such a case? Of course, let's buy another machine!

Okay, let's do it. Let's buy another B machine. But wait a minute—in our plant, there is only one person who has the skills to operate it. And this person already works 100 percent of the time. If the intention is not just to decorate the plant but to make more money, we have to hire another worker. Let's suppose we have found such a worker. Cheap. A real bargain. Just $400 per week, including fringe. We are facing now a more generic case. A decision to invest often impacts both operating expense and throughput. The company's operating expense has been raised to $6400 per week.

Now what is the question? We have purchased a new machine, we haven't gotten it as a gift. The purchase price of the machine is, let's say, $100,000. In order to simplify calculations, let's assume no interest. The question is, of course, how many weeks will it take to recover the price of the machine?

Again, I would strongly advise you to stop reading here, and do the calculation on your own. Not to test yourself, but to use this opportunity to reveal to yourself what actually guides your actions.

Very few of the people who have tackled this quiz were able to answer this last question correctly. The grip of the "cost world" is very much underestimated. Let's follow in their footsteps to track Western management's typical approach.

We have bought another B machine, so B is no longer the constraint. We can now supply all 100 P's, and all 50 Q's. We already have checked and there is sufficient capacity on all other resources. The market becomes the constraint.

P will bring us $100 \times 45 = 4500$ throughput dollars, and Q will bring an additional $50 \times 60 = 3000$ throughput dollars. The total throughput is $7500. From that, we will have to subtract the operating expense. Remember, it is now $6400; we have hired another person. The net profit is $1100 per week. But we cannot use all this money to recover the investment in the new machine. We were profitable before. We can only use the increase in the net profit that resulted from the purchase of the new machine.

The increase in net profit is $1100 - $300 = $800 more profit per week. Since the price of the machine was $100,000, we will recover the investment in exactly 125 weeks. Right? Wrong.

Let's remind ourselves of the fifth focusing step. IF IN THE PREVIOUS STEPS, A CONSTRAINT HAS BEEN BROKEN . . . This is exactly where we are, right? We have just broken a constraint . . . GO BACK TO STEP 1, BUT DO NOT ALLOW INERTIA TO CAUSE A SYSTEM'S CONSTRAINT. This warning is given for a situation like ours. Have we paid attention to it? You see, in the "cost world" almost everything is important, thus changing one or two things doesn't change the total picture much. But this is not the case in the "throughput world." Here, very few things are really important. Change one important thing and you must reevaluate the entire situation.

Why did we decide not to go to Japan? Because going to Japan would have yielded less than $2 per minute on the constraint. What constraint? We have already broken it! Purchasing the new machine created excess capacity on all resources. The market is now the only constraint. Let's go immediately to Japan and sell our excess capacity. The entire difference between selling price and raw-material price, the additional throughput, will be net profit. Operating expenses are fixed although now at a higher level.

If we go to Japan, what will become the internal constraint? What is the next resource in line? Resource A, of course. So let's redo the calculation. Selling 100 P's, domestically, will yield 4500 throughput dollars, but will require 1500 minutes on resource A. Fifty units of Q, sold domestically, will yield an additional 3000 throughput dollars, and require an additional 500 minutes from resource A. This leaves us with a surplus of 400 "idle" minutes on resource A. . . . Let's "dump" them in Japan.

How many P's can we produce in 400 minutes on resource A? About 26 units. The throughput per unit is not $45; we are selling in Japan. It is only $72 − $45 = 27 throughput dollars. So, selling P in Japan will add another 700 throughput dollars. Should we bother with such small amounts? Let's see. The total throughput now is $8200. Minus $6400 operating expense, minus the previous net profit of $300, brings the change in net profit to $1500 per week. Almost double the previous number. Because of INERTIA, we have left almost half of the money on the table.

Do we now understand the meaning of inertia? . . . Do we? Unfortunately the answer is still "No." In the "cost world" there is the concept of "product cost." As long as we haven't changed the product design or the workers' salaries, the "product cost" hasn't changed. But in the "throughput world" there is no such thing as "product cost" or "product profit." We have to evaluate the impact, not of a product, but of a decision. This evaluation must be done through the impact on the system's constraints. That's why identifying the constraints is always the first step. If the constraint has been changed, decisions have to be re-examined.

Why did we elect to sell P in Japan? Because we were under the impression that P was the most "profitable product." This impression is an extrapolation from the "cost world." "Profitable product" is yesterday's terminology. Yes, we had decided that it would be more profitable for the company to sell P. Why did we reach this conclusion? Because B was the constraint. But it is no longer the constraint.

Let's try to dump Q in Japan. Let's use the 400 residual minutes of A for the production of Q. We can produce 40 units, since Q requires only 10 minutes per unit of the constraint. The throughput of each Q sold in Japan is $80 (selling price in Japan is 20 percent lower), minus $40 for the raw materials, which equals $40 throughput dollars. Thus, selling Q in Japan will add an additional $1600 to net profit, rather than the $700 dollars gained by selling P. An increase of $900 to the bottom line. We are already going to Japan, why not sell the right product? INERTIA!

Do we now understand the meaning of inertia? Are we now fully aware of its devastating risks? The answer is still "No." Why did we decide that we had to squeeze everything domestically first, and only then examine the export possibility? Because initially export was not part of the picture. INERTIA!

GO BACK TO STEP ONE, DO NOT ALLOW INERTIA. Go back to step 1, and look on the system as if you have never seen it before. It IS a new system. Let's remind ourselves, once again, that in the "cost world," changing one or two items does not change much. In the "throughput world," changing a constraint changes everything.

What we have to do is re-examine which product contributes

more, through the constraint. The constraint now is A, not B. The way to calculate it was outlined before, throughput dollars divided by constraint minutes. Why don't you carry out the calculation, a surprise is waiting.

PART TWO

THE ARCHITECTURE OF AN INFORMATION SYSTEM

17. *Peering into the inherent structure of an information system—first attempt*

Information, as we realized earlier, is the answer to the question asked. What type of information are we looking for? To answer this question, we simply have to listen to everybody's complaint, "We are drowned in oceans of data; nevertheless, we lack information." Just listen carefully to the examples that follow this almost desperate cry. . . .

Should we accept this particular client order? Should we authorize that appropriation request for more machines? What offer should we submit for this bid? What else can we do to reduce the outrageous lead-times in product design? Should we make this particular part, or continue to purchase it? How can we objectively evaluate the performance of that local area? Which vendor should we choose? Etc., etc., etc.

It's hard to escape the realization that the most needed information relates to questions that cost accounting was supposed to answer. As a matter of fact, it's not surprising at all, since the decision process of the "cost world" is totally inappropriate for our reality of the "throughput world" . All these questions cannot be properly answered by our traditional decision-making procedures. Managers have had to rely only on their intuition. The bridge between data and the needed information—the decision process—was missing. Thus, the ocean of data we assem-

103

bled did not help to substantiate the intuitive answers. Actually, it just obliterated them.

Let's digest what we have just said, even at the risk of sounding somewhat redundant. This is a discussion, isn't it? It feels as if we are very close to finding the core, as if further talks will provide us with the base to define the nature of what we are seeking to find. The nature of the desired INFORMATION SYSTEMS is distinctly different from the available DATA SYSTEMS.

We have already noticed that information is arranged in a hierarchical structure, where information on a higher level can be deduced from the lower levels through the use of a decision procedure. We don't have the needed information, since we didn't use the appropriate decision procedures. This implies that the information system we are looking for should be mainly geared to higher levels of information. Interesting conclusion! Let's dig a little bit deeper.

Whenever the question could be answered without involving a decision procedure, strictly by capturing the required data, we have already done it. That is where most of our past efforts have been channeled. No wonder we call our current systems DATA SYSTEMS. Not that we didn't try to answer higher level questions; the list of questions that we outlined above was always before our eyes—COST systems are a very good example of our past attempts. But as we discovered in our discussion, since these efforts were based on an erroneous decision process, they led us nowhere.

Given this situation, we should reserve the words INFORMATION SYSTEMS for systems that are able to answer questions which require the utilization of a decision procedure. Systems that are geared to answer most straightforward questions, should be called DATA SYSTEMS. This last decision implies that an information system should not be consumed in dealing with available data, but should assume the existence of a data system and should suck the required data from it. A far-reaching conclusion, but not counter-intuitive.

The power of an information system should be judged mainly

on the scope of the questions it can reliably answer. The wider the scope, the more powerful the system.

Where do we go from here? It seems as if the first step is to develop the appropriate decision procedures for each of the above-mentioned questions—and for many more that have not been mentioned.

This, as you no doubt suspect, guarantees that our little discussion will have to continue for quite some time, certainly beyond the scope of just this book. Even one small quiz was sufficient to demonstrate that it won't be boring, but can we afford the time now? If we follow this track, when will we discuss the structure of an INFORMATION SYSTEM?

The temptation to construct the various decision procedures is very big, especially as we start to realize that these new procedures are not very complicated or exorbitantly sophisticated. On the contrary, they are embarrassingly simple. No wonder; when we replace the notion that almost everything is important with the realization that only a few things really count, then things are marvelously simplified. We have already noticed that the "cost world" mentality is so deeply ingrained in us that it masks reality. It is certainly going to be fun to knock down so many mental blocks, devising those long, desperately needed procedures. But . . .

But let's not forget the main purpose of this discussion. It was to outline the structure and composition of a comprehensive and reliable INFORMATION SYSTEM. Can we do it without first devising all the required decision procedures?

Luckily, we have already established the guidelines to derive decision procedures to answer managerial questions. They are simply the FIVE FOCUSING STEPS. Maybe we can find the structure of the required INFORMATION SYSTEM by examining just one or two such managerial questions. Maybe there is a generic pattern. If this is the case, we can build the framework now and gradually fill it in as we deal with each type of specific question. In this way we can start to reap major benefits much earlier. Besides, we will have to introduce those concepts into our organizations in a gradual way anyhow. The full transition from the COST WORLD to the THROUGHPUT WORLD is not going to happen in one short day.

Well, what are we waiting for? Let's start.

Suppose that you are the purchasing manager. One of your major problems is to determine the levels of raw-material inventories that you have to hold for each item. You know this ungrateful job. If you don't hold enough inventory, operations will run into shortages and everyone will be on your back. If you try to build some real reserves, the controller will send your boss to hammer some sense into you. How much should you hold? And not less important, how can you prove that you are holding inventories at the right level?

Let's examine your problem using some specific figures. Suppose that the purchase price of one item is $100 per unit and the vendor lead-time is six months. Another item can be bought for $1000 per unit and the vendor lead-time is only two months. How many weeks of inventory should you hold for each item?

Don't be too hasty in your answer. It's the perception of the "cost world" that will lead you to believe that the answer is obvious; that the inventory levels of the first part should be higher than the levels of the second part. In the last five years we have learned that other factors are much more dominant than the price and the vendor lead-time. Let's consider one of these additional factors.

If we are debating what the stock levels should be, it means that the these items are consumed on an on-going basis, not sporadically. Otherwise, we would have purchased just enough to meet specific orders and would not consider holding raw-material stocks. So, let's suppose that the frequency of delivery of the first item is one delivery every other week, while the frequency of the second item is just one delivery per month. What is your answer now? Which item should have the higher inventory level?

We should hold about two weeks inventory of the first item, two weeks of our consumption. But for the second item, two weeks certainly will not be sufficient. We should hold about one month. Right?

Where do price and vendor lead-time enter the picture? Are they important at all? Yes, but to a much less extent than we had thought. You see, when we say one month of consumption, what do we really mean? One month's average consumption? We are a little bit more experienced than that. We are painfully aware that Murphy is the most active person in our company. We should hold one month of "paranoia consumption." To what extent should we be paranoid?

Our paranoia is, of course, a function of the internal fluctuations, which in turn are heavily influenced by the fluctuation in our clients' demands. How can we quantify paranoia, or alternatively, quantify Murphy? That's another question. Nevertheless, it is obvious that our degree of paranoia will be influenced by the unit price of the item. The higher the price the less we can afford to be paranoid. Amazing, isn't it? Something that we considered to be the most important parameter in the "cost world," turns out to be just a correction factor in the "throughput world."

What about vendor lead-time? Is it important at all? Once again, yes, but just as a secondary corrective factor. When we issue an order to a vendor, which we must do at least the vendor lead-time ahead of delivery, we should consider not our current "paranoia consumption" but our future "paranoia consumption." The material that we order today will serve as stock only after it arrives at our company, an event that we hope will take place in the vendor lead-time from issuing the order.

For example, for the first item, we will have to evaluate what the consumption will be six months down the road. Of course, the longer the vendor lead-time, the more remote the future time-frame that has to be evaluated, and thus the uncertainty increases. But let's not forget that the item price and the vendor lead-times are still much less important than the frequency of delivery. They impact the result just through the level of the noise caused by internal fluctuations. The more stable our own company, the less important they are.

Talking about levels of noise, we need to recognize that our own company is not the only one bringing uncertainty to the game. Unreliability of the vendor is also important. Let's use the same case, and assume that the first vendor, the one that delivers every two weeks, is very unreliable. Unreliable to the extent that there is a considerable chance that he will skip a delivery or two, or that a whole shipment will be defective. The other vendor is extremely reliable, both in the shipment dates and the material quality. What are the answers now? Do you remember the question? It was, "What levels of inventories should we hold for each item?"

We see that in determining raw-material inventory levels, three major factors have to be considered. The first is the frequency of delivery, the second, our own company noise (the unreliability in consumption levels). The third factor is vendor reliability (both in meeting delivery dates and in the quality of the products). This last realization raises another important question: if one vendor is offering better prices, the second better frequency, and the third higher reliability, which vendor would you choose? The need for a numerical evaluation is quite obvious.

What have we done, besides demonstrating once again the difference between thinking logically in the throughput world, rather than playing the number game of the cost world? Can we learn from this last example anything that will help us in revealing the needed structure of an information system?

18. *Introducing the need to quantify "protection"*

We can learn quite a bit about the structure of the desired IN-FORMATION SYSTEM from the last example. We just have to refuse to panic. As a matter of fact, it is not as complicated as it might seem. Where did our analysis regarding managerial purchasing issues end? The question of proper raw-material inventory levels, as well as the question of selecting vendors, was strongly dependent on one piece of required data: our level of "paranoia consumption."

If we knew that illusive piece of data, we could have, without a lot of hassle, used the other pieces to arrive at a reasonable numerical judgement. How should we go about getting this data? The first question that we should ask ourselves is quite clear. What determines the consumption rate?

The first impression is that this question can be answered, at least conceptually, without any hesitation. The system's constraints determine the rate of consumption. Are we sure? Just the system's constraints? Given a set of constraints, are there any additional degrees of freedom in determining the consumption rate?

OK, I see what you mean. The constraints should determine the consumption rate, but improper decisions on how to consider them can drastically effect the end result. If, on one hand,

109

we don't utilize the constraints properly, the consumption rate will be less than desired. On the other hand, if we ignore them and concentrate instead on artificial "labor efficiencies," raw-material consumption rates will be unnecessarily inflated.

It looks like a *déjà vu,* as if we are following a very known and beaten path. What we just verbalized is a repeat of the focusing steps. First we need to IDENTIFY the system's constraints. Then to decide how to EXPLOIT them and SUBORDINATE to them. Makes sense, and not so surprising. Does the need to SUBORDINATE enter only through the need to erase the tendency to achieve high efficiencies? No, not necessarily so—let's not forget that we need to predict not consumption but the "paranoia consumption." Can it be achieved? Of course, but for this purpose we have to develop an additional mechanism.

Remember, why are we "paranoid" to start with? Because we are well aware that things usually do not go smoothly. Disturbances are part of life. Thus we need to develop a mechanism that will predict, numerically, the levels of inventory required throughout the company, given the patterns of constraints and the noise level in our company. Yes, the subordinating step is very dominant here.

What we see, at least in this case, is that to answer a managerial question, even where the decision process is fully developed and understood (which, I suspect, is not yet the case here) we need data. This type of data is not available in the "cost world." It is information at a lower level, information that the traditional decision procedures were incapable of deducing from the readily available data. We see that before we can reliably answer such purchasing questions, two preliminary steps must be carried out by our information system.

The first step that our information system will have to include is the procedure necessary to IDENTIFY and EXPLOIT the constraints and SUBORDINATE everything else to them—now and in the future. This step (or block of code if we consider a computerized information system), must be put in place. On top of this, a second step must be instituted, a step based on a procedure to distill the noise level from the actual daily transactions occurring in our company. This procedure must be able to translate this data into proper protection levels to be placed at appropriate locations to minimize the impact of Murphy.

Let's examine another very common question to see whether the same pattern repeats itself. If our FIVE FOCUSING STEPS are as generic as we suspect they are, this must be the case.

Suppose that we are currently purchasing a certain item which we have the technical capability to make in-house. Should we continue to purchase it or should we start to produce it? The "cost world" answer is (on the face of it) ridiculous. What are we supposed to do? Calculate the "cost to produce" the item and compare it to the purchase price? Suppose that the "cost to produce" in-house is $100 (according to traditional calculations) and the purchase cost is $80. Then what?

By now we have learned our lesson. The "product cost" is just a mathematical phantom, with no relevance to real life. The easiest way to substantiate this claim is by examining the situation described above with the following additional data. Suppose the purchase price of the raw material needed to produce this given item is $40, and that all internal efforts are done only by non-constraints. Now, what is your answer? Purchasing the item will negatively impact the bottom line by $80, while producing it in-house will negatively impact it by . . . yes, only $40.

OK, the need to identify the system's constraints is obvious. What about the second step, the EXPLOIT concept? Maybe the decision to bring the part in-house is actually the utilization of this concept, even though a reverse mode to the one we have used so far. Makes sense. And the third step, the SUBORDINATION concept? We might say that since the decision was made at the second step, the third step has no effect.

We might say this, but it is wrong. We should understand the subject of SUBORDINATION in much more depth. Let's remember that most of our understanding of the application of the five focusing steps has been derived, so far, from the quiz.

One of the basic assumptions on which the quiz was built is the absence of any uncertainty, of noise. This was done, if you recall, in order to put to bed, once and for all, the common excuses: the notion that what prevents us from achieving information is mainly data uncertainty. It's a very good reason to omit noise, but it has also blocked us from an in-depth examination of the SUBORDINATION mechanism.

In SUBORDINATION, attention is focused on the "stronger links" of our chain. Yes, we realized that in any chain there must be only one "weakest link." But why does this phenomenon exist? We can rigorously prove that it must be the case in any system that contains both dependent variables and statistical fluctuations. If a material will cross, in its journey through our company, more than one internal physical constraint, the expected throughput will not be achieved and inventory will climb indefinitely. (For details see *Theory of Constraints Journal,* Volume 1, Issue 5, Article No. 1).

In other words, we should avoid interactive constraints as we would avoid the plague. This last conclusion leads us to realize that all other "links" must have more capacity than is strictly predicted by the expected load. It's all very nice and logical, but what is the simple, common-sense reason for it? If mathematics shows that this is actually the situation, we must accept it, but the question still remains. Why does this phenomenon exist? Maybe the answer is simply our well-known but undesirable friend Mr. Murphy?

Let's look into it, bearing in mind what we have learned so far. Suppose that we have identified a system's constraint; we now want to exploit it. Any waste of the constraint will irreversibly jeopardize our bottom line. But wait, we just remembered the existence of Murphy. If Murphy hits the constraint directly, too bad. It seems that the only thing to do is curse our bad luck and continue on. But if Murphy hits one of the resources feeding the constraint, are we as helpless?

We would like to still EXPLOIT the constraint itself. This we can do, provided that we have prepared, beforehand, some inventory in front of our constraint. Seems like a good idea; the inventory that we need to protect our throughput is certainly not going to be considered a liability—as long as Murphy exists, we'd better have it.

But is inventory itself sufficient protection? When Murphy hits, and we continue to exploit the constraint, it will eat into the inventory that we accumulated in front of it. Then what? Murphy is not an infrequent visitor in our companies. What happens when Murphy hits the non-constraints again? The constraint is now exposed.

It is obvious that we'd better hurry to rebuild the inventory placed before the constraint, build it up again before "Murphy strikes again." But in order do so, all the non-constraints must be able to process material faster than is strictly demanded by the rate of the constraint. They have to continue to supply what the constraint needs plus rebuild the protective inventory. This brings us to the unavoidable conclusion that as long as statistical fluctuations exist, if we want to exploit the constraint, all other resources must have more capacity than is strictly dictated by the demand.

To clarify it further, let's pretend that one of the feeding resources does not have any spare capacity. In such a case, what level of inventory do we need in front of the constraint to guarantee that we can always exploit it? Suppose that Murphy strikes this particular resource or any resource feeding it. The constraint will then have to eat into its inventory, and there is no way now to replenish it. The level of protection is permanently lowered. Now Murphy strikes once more. Again the level of protective inventory drops. And on and on . . . As long as we accept that Murphy does not go away, how much inventory should we initially place in front of the constraint? Yes, if we do have another constraint in the chain—a resource having no spare capacity—we need infinite inventory to be able to exploit even one constraint.

A constraint, because it cannot afford any internal protective capacity, must be shielded against Murphy by a combination of inventory placed right in front of it and the protective capacity of the resources feeding it. There is a trade-off between these two protection mechanisms. Less protective capacity in the feeding resources will require higher levels of inventory in front of the constraint. Otherwise, the constraint will be starved from time to time and throughput for the entire company will be lost. If one of the resources has zero protective capacity, the required inventory in front of the downstream constraint must be infinite.

Thus, if a chain has more than one weakest link, its strength will be considerably less than even the strength of each of its weakest links. Such a chain will be torn quickly by reality; systems containing interactive constraints are just transient in our fierce world.

We used to consider as waste any available capacity which is higher than what is strictly needed for production. Now, we realize that when we examine available capacity, we have to distinguish between three, rather than two, conceptual capacity segments. The first is productive capacity, the segment that we need for actual production to meet demand. The second segment is protective capacity, which is needed as a shield against Murphy. Only the constraint resource does not have protective capacity (remember—EXPLOIT). Any capacity remaining after we take into account productive and protective capacities is actually excess capacity.

Now we see that when we bring a purchased item in-house, it might have a negative impact, even if all the required production is done by non-constraint resources. For example, if the item needs the time of a non-constraint resource that currently does not have any excess capacity, the additional load will, by definition, eat into that resource's protective capacity. This will necessitate an increase in work-in-process and finished-goods inventory levels, to protect the constraints. An increase in the inventories, not just of the new item, but of every other item that crosses these same areas.

This is a totally new consideration, which we haven't taken into account thus far. You see, in our quiz we concentrated only on the impact on throughput and operating expense. What we should do is always evaluate the impact on all three measurements, inventory included. The subordination step is essential in reliably answering make-buy questions.

Let's remind ourselves that the reason for placing INVENTORY second on the scale of importance was the indirect impact of inventory on throughput. If we want to get a quantitative answer for the impact of an action (even just on net profit), we cannot possibly ignore inventory. For many questions, it might even be the dominant factor.

Moreover, this business of "protective capacity" immediately raises the question of how do we distinguish between this mysterious protective capacity and ordinary excess capacity? How do we know, when a resource is idle, whether it's OK or it's just a waste?

These last two important issues raise, once again, the requirement that our INFORMATION SYSTEM not only IDENTIFY and EXPLOIT the constraints but also distill from the actual events in our company some means for determining the level of Murphy.

The same exact conclusion as before. Maybe now we should try to pin down the architecture of an information system.

19. *Required data can be achieved only through scheduling and quantification of Murphy*

What we should now concentrate on is sketching a block diagram of the overall architecture of the desired information system.

The content of the highest block is crystal clear. Any information system that lives up to its name must be able to answer the types of WHAT IFs listed in the previous chapters. That's what we really want, isn't it? Try to imagine the impact that having reliable answers to such questions will have on our company. Especially in light of the fact that currently we are consistently deriving erroneous, almost opposite, answers.

But even the first examination revealed to us that in order to achieve this end, other blocks are needed. The data which is required for the WHAT IF phase is simply unavailable. It is sufficient to re-examine what we have already done to get a very good idea of the types of data that are missing. As a matter of fact, we can start to distinguish between two types of missing data.

The first one sticks out like a sore thumb—knowledge of what are the company's constraints. We must develop the procedure to identify current and future constraints. Moreover, it must have the ability to identify what the constraints will be if we choose a particular alternative, one of the alternatives that we evaluate in our WHAT IF stage.

As we mentioned before, constraints are not necessarily physical; many times they are constraining policies. An IN-FORMATION SYSTEM should concentrate on physical constraints and not yield to the stupidity of instituting devastating policy constraints.

How can we IDENTIFY the system's constraints? We should realize that some constraints can be found right at the start—like resource B in our quiz. Other constraints can be found only after the EXPLOITATION step has been completed on the already identified constraints—like the case of market potential for product P. Some other constraints may be revealed only after subordination is done. This is usually the case for resources that do not have enough protective capacity.

From the above, it's clear that all constraints cannot be found simultaneously; there is no one all-encompassing step. We'll have to do it gradually, maybe even by going through the first three steps in an iterative process, where an additional constraint is identified at each loop. Since the number of constraints is very small, this fact, by itself, does not represent a significant burden.

But something else begins to dawn on us. Some constraints can be found only after the subordination stage has been done, subordination to the already identified and exploited constraint. If that's the case, then the only way not to go through the iterative process in real life is to simulate future events.

This is a very important and quite surprising conclusion. What we just said is that in order to identify even the CUR-RENT constraints, we need to simulate FUTURE actions. To identify constraints, an information system must have the ability to simulate future actions. This means that an integral and fundamental part of our INFORMATION SYSTEM is SCHEDULING.

It seems as if we are encountering another long-standing need, the ability to systematically generate a reliable schedule. Yes, that's it, no doubt. SCHEDULE must be one of the building blocks of an information system. A block which is a prerequisite to the WHAT IF block.

At first, this conclusion seems as if we have to carry an additional burden. We would like to reach the stage where we can answer managerial questions, and now we face the huge barrier of constructing a reliable schedule for our resources. On second thought, it should not surprise us. For a long time, some of the most burning managerial questions have been: "What should we release to the process?" "When should we release it?" "In what quantities should we do things?" In short: who should do what, when, and in what quantities?—SCHEDULING.

Scheduling is actually a list of answers to managerial questions and as such it is information. Do we need a decision process in order to generate this information? Remember, this was our acid test to distinguish between what should be included in an information system or left for a data system.

Well, can we generate a reliable schedule without a decision process? The answer is, most probably, no. You see, nobody has a reliable scheduling system; it is certainly not readily available data. This must be because the current attempts are based on an erroneous decision process.

Maybe scheduling information is not available because people have not really tried? This is definitely not the case. It is sufficient to realize how much money, time, and effort have been, and still are being, invested in the attempts to install and operate MRP (Material Resource Planning) systems.

The original thrust for implementing MRP was, and still is, scheduling. Almost no company, that I'm aware of, implemented MRP just to get a data base. Today a great many industrial companies have already installed (some more than just once) such a system. If we take into account not just the price of the software, the hardware, and the expensive implementation, but also the horrendous on-going price of maintaining the data in a semi-accurate stage, it's hard to escape reaching an estimate of many billions. Not having a reliable, systematic mode of scheduling is certainly not because of lack of effort.

Enough said. Whether or not we like it, if we want to get

reliable answers to managerial questions, we'll have to crack the problem of reliable scheduling. SCHEDULING is definitely one of the basic blocks of an information system, but unfortunately not the only additional block that we need.

Our explorations have revealed the vast importance of the role that Murphy plays in our companies. Just re-read the previous chapter, and you will realize that Murphy is actually the reason we need inventory and protective capacity to satisfy the current throughput. How can we measure Murphy?

To try and measure the local perturbations on each individual resource is not only a mammoth task, it is theoretically an impossibility. Simply, the time required to assemble enough statistics is, in reality, much longer than the mean time between changes. The only way out seems to be to look at the aggregated impact of all of Murphy's "actions."

What do we need to protect against Murphy? The system's constraints. The additional inventory is accumulated in front of the constraint, so if something goes wrong upstream, the constraint can continue to be exploited without any interruption. (Remember, the market is almost always a physical constraint in systems where we assume no policy constraints). The protective capacity on the feeding non-constraints must be there in order to catch up after Murphy has struck. The inventory protection should be restored to a sufficient level before Murphy strikes again.

The few places where the impact of all Murphy's actions aggregate is now clearly spotted: it is the inventory accumulations right before the constraints. This is the logical basis for the procedure that we call BUFFER MANAGEMENT.

Here, I don't think that we should expand too much on this interesting procedure. As a matter of fact, my opinion is that we should restrain ourselves from diving into any particular procedure, no matter how interesting and important it might seem, before we firmly establish the conceptual design of an information system. Otherwise, we run the risk of never reaching our main target. Once the overall framework is built, then, and only then, it will be time to expand and describe in detail each procedure as we encounter the need.

Nevertheless, we cannot leave the subject of BUFFER MANAGEMENT without clarifying some of its fundamental terminology. First of all, it is quite unfair just to mention a procedure and depart, leaving us wondering what really happened. The second and probably more important reason is that if you don't define fundamental terminology, it has a nasty habit of popping up in unexpected places, turning everything into confusing unopened knots. But for this purpose we need a new chapter.

20. *Introducing the time buffer concept*

Let's go back to the issue of buffers. We said that we need to build buffers of inventory before the constraints. Wait a minute, maybe we jumped the gun a little too fast. What we really said was that we have to protect our ability to exploit the constraint. Isn't it the same thing? Not necessarily. A physical constraint might not be a resource, it might be the market, or if we want to be more specific, a client order.

So what?

If we want to guarantee on-time delivery in spite of the problems that Murphy causes, it looks as if the only solution is to build finished-goods inventories. Isn't that so?

Not always. Suppose that the agreements that we have with our clients call for deliveries no later than specific dates; we are not allowed to ship later, but if we ship earlier our clients are very happy. Yes, granted that this is not always the case, but certainly this type of situation is very common. In cases where we have the latitude of shipping earlier, are finished-goods stocks the only way to protect on-time delivery?

Once the question is asked in this way, it is apparent that we can protect the desired due-date with inventory or with time. We can start the fulfillment of an order, not at the time mandated by the duration of the processes involved, but at an earlier time. Starting earlier than required will allow sufficient time to react to unexpected disturbances, and ensure on-time deliv-

121

ery. If no misfortune happens, we will finish the order ahead of
the promised date, but the result will not be finished goods, it
will be an early shipment.

Re-examining what we just said leaves a somewhat unpleasant taste in the mouth—as if we are just playing with words.
Yes, we can protect by inventory, or as we saw in the last example, we can protect by the action of pre-release, by time. Time
and inventory are not synonymous. Still, we feel as if we have
said the same thing twice.

Where does this uneasy feeling stem from? Maybe we should
deal with the case where clients will not accept an early shipment; a case where it is obvious that the only way to protect is
by building finished-goods inventory. So how are we going to
build those inventories? By starting operations earlier than
strictly needed. It means that in both cases the real actions will
be exactly the same: we achieve the protection by an early start.
Are we dealing with two protection mechanisms or just one?

Maybe the best way to find out is by examining another case,
where the constraint is a resource constraint. This is the case
where our intuition is most developed. Here it is clear that we
must make sure that protective inventory is built in front of the
constraint. How do we make sure that such protective inventory is built? Think in terms of a job-shop, in terms of many
different products moving through the same constraint. The
way to build inventory is the same as before, to start the production of each task earlier than is strictly dictated by the process and movement times.

Why is it that two different entities, time and inventory, appear to be one when judged by the actions that they imply? I
believe that this uniformity stems from the fact that these two
protective mechanisms must exist at the same time. Actually,
it's not two protective mechanisms, but one. The duality stems
from the different points of view by which we tend to look on
things. We might say that there are two different things that we
are trying to protect. One is the constraint, the other is the
output of the constraint—the client orders.

If we use the terminology of protecting the constraint itself, the focus is on making sure that the constraint will not be idle. The terminology that we will naturally use is that of INVEN-TORY; the specific inventory composition is not relevant. Ac-tually, what do we call "protecting the constraint" if it's not protecting its output? If we concentrate on the output of the constraint, the specific client's orders, then the terminology that we'll naturally use is TIME.

As we said, protecting the constraint or protecting the output of a constraint is basically the same thing, and thus it is no wonder that the derived actions are identical—pre-release. But which terminology should we use in the future, inventory or time? It looks as if we are facing a choice, but as we learned so many times in the past, arbitrary choices are just the result of insufficient understanding. So, why don't we spend a little more time to clarify the issue, rather than choosing in haste and fac-ing a fifty percent chance of regretting it bitterly down the road.

What did we say? If we use the terminology of protecting the constraint, we tend to use inventory as the protection mecha-nism. The specific identity of the inventory composition is of no relevance. Interesting. Can it be that the composition of the inventory is not relevant? Sounds fishy. Let's peer more deeply into it. "Protect the constraint." Where did this phrase come from? Actually it is a shortened version of the second focusing step: Decide how to EXPLOIT the system's constraints. Now it is quite obvious, isn't it?

If exploiting the constraint means make it work continu-ously, then the composition of the inventory is of no relevance. But this is not the case. Exploit the constraint means make the most out of it (in terms of the predetermined goal). Our famous quiz has already taught us that the key lies in the content of the work we choose to activate the constraint on. Only when we deal with one single product does the meaning of EXPLOIT deteriorate to "make it work all the time."

Since the composition of the content of the constraint's work is of utmost importance, the protection must be expressed as TIME. This determination (not a choice any more) is also in line with our intuition when we regard broader applications than just production. Projects, design engineering, administration, not to mention service sectors, all belong to the realm of our discussion. They all deal with tasks that have to be fulfilled by resources in order to achieve a predetermined goal. But in those environments, inventory is often invisible, where TIME is always very well understood.

We have decided to use TIME as our unit of protection, and thus whenever we refer to buffer we are actually referring to TIME BUFFER. The buffer is thus an interval of time—the interval of time that we release the task prior to the time that we would have released it if we assumed that Murphy did not exist. Buffers are expressed in hours, days, or months.

What determines the length of a buffer?

2   The probability of overcoming a disturbancy at one particular resource as a function of the time it takes.

TIME BUFFER is our protection against unknown disturbances. What is unknown in them is not that they will occur; their occurrence is almost given. What we don't know is when will they occur, where will they hit, and for how long the disruption will last. Due to the stochastic nature of disturbances, it is obvious that we are not in a position to determine the time buffer precisely. Even if we have the time and resources to assemble all the statistical data, we will just end up with a probability curve. Such a curve is shown in Figure 2, where in twenty percent of the cases the disturbance lasts five minutes, and in one percent of the cases the disturbance lasts two days.

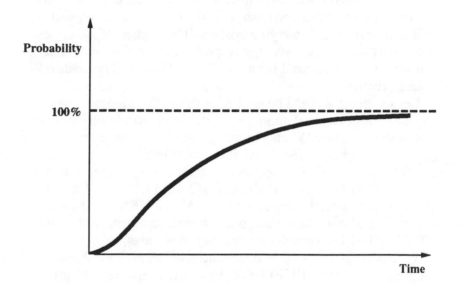

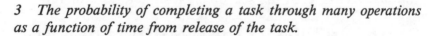

3   The probability of completing a task through many operations as a function of time from release of the task.

We can gain more knowledge from such a graph by looking on its integral. That will tell us the probability of overcoming the disturbance within a given period of time. But we will gain much more if we'll look on the impact it has on the duration of completing a task through several activities. Figure 3 represents the probability of completing a task as a function of the time elapsed from its release. Notice that this curve never reaches the 100% probability. As we move to longer and longer time intervals the probability of overcoming disturbances increases, but it never reaches certainty.

Determining the length of the TIME BUFFER is a judgment call, and it's not an easy or trivial task. If we want to be super cautious and choose a very long buffer, we can safely accommodate almost any disturbance, but at what price? Our lead times will be a priori very long—we will release materials much earlier than we can use them. The average levels of work-in-process and finished-goods inventories will be inflated. As a result, we increase our need for cash, our future competitive position will deteriorate, and carrying costs will be higher. If we choose very short buffers, our average response time will be very quick, but we must be prepared for a lot of expediting and quite unreliable deliveries.

Let's stress it again. The setting of the buffer's length involves the most fundamental managerial decision—trade-off between the measurements. When choosing long buffers it directly impacts the level of time-related INVENTORY (work-in-process and finished-tasks). Consequently it indirectly impacts future THROUGHPUT and OPERATING EXPENSES. Choosing short buffers directly impacts OPERATING EXPENSES (expediting and control) and once again, current and future THROUGHPUT (unreliable delivery due-dates).

Who should make this decision, who should establish the length of the TIME BUFFERS? In most companies it's not the top manager or even the scheduler, it's the forklift driver.

THE DECISION ON THE LENGTH OF THE BUFFERS MUST BE IN THE HANDS OF THE PEOPLE DIRECTLY RESPONSIBLE FOR THE OVERALL PERFORMANCE OF THE COMPANY.

21. *Buffers and buffer-origins*

As we have seen, more detailed statistical data will not help make a better decision. If we want to reduce the room for trade-offs we have to deal directly with the core reason for the need for protection—Murphy. In close examination we can see that there are two types of Murphy. One involves unexpected changes, like a tool breakdown, a worker who does not show up today, or an out-of-control process that causes scrap. This is the way we usually envision Murphy. I call this type of disruption "Pure Murphy." But when we look on the flow of a specific product, rather than on the resources, we notice another type of disruption.

When a particular task arrives at a non-constraint resource, a resource which has enough protective capacity, nevertheless we might find that the resource is busy working on another needed task. The flow of our task is disrupted. The task will have to wait in the resource's queue. This phenomenon is well known to everybody who has worked in an organization. I call it NON-INSTANT AVAILABILITY.

To better understand this situation, let's establish some general relationships between the intervals of time involved in determining the lead time. It is estimated that in most environments disturbances are the overwhelming factor in determining the task's lead time. The actual task's process time is, almost always, negligible compared to the impact of Murphy. For production tasks most companies have the data to support this assertion.

Take a moment and estimate the actual process time needed for one average part. No, don't consider a product, we process and assemble its parts in parallel. Consider one typical PART. Once again! Don't take the most complicated part, take the average one. Whoops, not the time to process an entire batch, just a single unit. Remember, except for very unique processes, we can move a part to the next step in the process before the batch has been completed at the previous step. (When we are expediting we call it "splitting and overlapping" of batches. In TOC terminology it is simply the difference between the "process batch" and the "transfer batch.") If you are not a supplier of involved aerospace parts, the average process time per unit is probably less than an hour, and in semi-process industries it's just seconds.

Now let's compare it to the average time that we hold this inventory in our possession. How are we going to figure out that number? Quite simple. You probably have, or can get, a relatively good estimation on the work-in-process and finished-goods inventory turns. Twelve inventory turns a year means that a company is holding, on average, every piece (from release to shipment) for about one month. Compare the previous number, which is probably expressed in minutes, to this number which is probably expressed in weeks. The actual process time is negligible compared to Murphy.

The lead-time of tasks is dominated by Murphy. For all practical purposes the TIME BUFFER is the time interval by which we predate the release of work, relative to the date at which the corresponding constraint's consumption is scheduled. There is (in most cases) no need to bother with the negligible correction of the time needed to actually do the job on the resources themselves.

What about the two types of disturbances, "pure Murphy" and "non-instant availability"? Which one of these is more dominant in determining the buffer length? I don't know. Until very recently, due to lack of a comprehensive information system, there was no practical way to separate them in reality. Still there is simply not enough real-life experience to answer this question rigorously. My personal guess is that they are roughly comparable, but only time will tell.

The choice of TIME, rather than INVENTORY, as the basic unit of protection may seem so natural that you probably wonder, why are we spending so much time on the obvious. But wait, some of the ramifications are almost counter-intuitive. We are accustomed to BUFFERS as physical things. For example, nobody will raise eyebrows when hearing a question like "Where are the buffers located?" or "How much inventory is stored in the buffers?" But now, can we continue using such terminology? Not anymore.

If a buffer is an interval of time, we can no longer talk in terms of buffer location or buffer content. Time does not have a location or content. We thus must introduce a new term that will enable us to refer to the location where the inventory will tend to accumulate due to the early release.

Why? For two reasons. One is that these locations are very important because it is the location where we can start to track the aggregated impact of all disturbances. This consideration has led Eli Shragenhaim to suggest the term "buffer checking point."

The second reason does not relate to the use of the buffers but to the process by which we insert them into our plans. As we said, BUFFER is an interval of time. How do we place this floating time interval on the time axis?

If we just think about it for a moment, we will see that there is only one choice. The buffers are there to protect the performance of the constraints. Thus, whenever we decide that a constraint has to perform a task at a specific time, we have to release the needed "material" a buffer before that point in time. ("Material" appears in quotation marks, since it might not necessarily be physical materials. It might be drawings or even permission to start design.)

We just said that in order to determine the "material" release date, we have to move buffer time backwards in time from the date on which the constraint is supposed to start consumption. This is the way we "nail" the time intervals expressed by the buffers into the action plan. Or another way to express it: to determine the release schedule, we have to attach the end of the time buffers to the schedule of the future consumption of the constraint.

On the time axis the schedule of consumption of the constraints is the ORIGIN of the time buffers. The time buffer stretches backward in time from this point. Let's remind ourselves that we are dealing here only with physical constraints. Policy constraints should not be buffered, they should be elevated. The physical constraints, either a resource or an order, do have a location, and thus we can refer to the locations from which the constraints consume the needed "materials" as BUFFER-ORIGIN. This terminology enables us to mentally connect the buffers—which are time intervals—to the physical location where the resulting protective inventory accumulations accrue.

Before we can drop this subject we still have to clarify one important issue; how many types of BUFFERS—and thus BUFFER-ORIGINS—do we have in a company?

From what we said so far it is quite obvious that we have more than one type of buffer-origin, because we have more than one type of physical constraint. We have to protect our resource constraints, since we don't want their work to be interrupted; this will necessitate a RESOURCE BUFFER. The buffer-origin of the resource buffer is the area right in front of that resource constraint, and it contains work-in-process inventories.

We also have to protect the market constraints, as we want to ship on time. This will necessitate a SHIPPING BUFFER. The buffer-origin is simply the shipping dock or the finished-goods warehouse. Notice, in cases where early shipments are allowed, the buffer-origin of the shipping buffer does not necessarily contain finished-goods inventory. It contains the list of orders that were shipped prior to their due dates.

Are these the only two buffer types? I suspect it will behoove us to introduce a third type of buffer, the ASSEMBLY

BUFFER. To clarify this recommendation, let's examine a case where a resource constraint is feeding one part to an assembly. This assembly operation assembles that part with other types of parts which are produced only by non-constraints. We don't want the part fed by the resource constraint to wait in front of assembly for parts done only by non-constraints. Remember, the basic concept is to EXPLOIT the constraint.

Allowing the work of the constraint to be delayed from becoming throughput, just because of non-constraints, is certainly remote from the ideal case of exploit. If we want to "guarantee" that the constraint's part will not wait, we have to bring all other parts prior to its expected time of arrival. In other words, we have to pre-release all other non-constraints' parts. The need for the ASSEMBLY BUFFER is almost self-evident. The buffer-origin of the assembly buffer will be placed only in front of assemblies that use at least one part fed by a constraint. This type of buffer-origin will contain only non-constraint parts.

Now that we have clarified some of the basic terminology, let's outline in broad terms the structure of this second basic block, the basic block of our information system that deals primarily with Murphy, with disturbances.

22. *First step in quantifying Murphy*

We have clarified the relevant terminology, now we should use it for its main purpose—the quantification of disturbances. Maybe the way to start is, once again, by digging to the roots. Maybe, we should start by exposing the basic approach to Murphy, which stems from our concept of time buffers. It is somewhat different from the traditional approach, nor does it coincide with the one preached by Total Quality Management (TQM). It is, in a way, a blend of the two.

In the not too distant past, the traditional way to treat Murphy, although we hate to admit it, was by accepting his existence and buffering almost every single task with inventory and time. What were the usual "explanations" for the existence of mounting finished goods? Usually, any attempt to peer into it encountered aggressive questions like: "What will happen if an urgent client order comes over the phone tomorrow? What are we going to do then? Tell him to wait for two weeks? We'll lose the order!"

Or there was the traditional response to the suggestion to restrain non-constraint resources from producing continuously. Do you recall how such a suggestion was encountered—of course, once the local managers were convinced that it was not a joke, that we meant it seriously? "And what will we do if a machine breaks down?" "Yes, we do have spare time now, but tomorrow anything can happen." As a matter of fact you and I know, too well, that every worker, engineer, secretary, or manager feels safe only if there is a pile of work waiting for them.

This type of approach is definitely devastating. No wonder that Total Quality Management zealously attacks it. "Don't accept Murphy, he is not an act of God, concentrate on eliminating problems!" That is their main message. Some TQM advocates have gone as far as putting on their flag the statement: "Do it right the first time." They are not saying "Never make a mistake"; they are warning against repeating the same mistakes over and over again. They don't expect a prototype to work perfectly the first time. They are trying to change the current mind-set. If the same type of batch is done over and over, why should we calmly accept that the first few items in a batch will always be defective?

Even though we full-heartedly support this fierce message, nevertheless, the approach we have chosen is much more moderate. Our starting point is quite different. We fully realize that in our real life Murphy cannot be eliminated. Yes, fighting Murphy is a very worthwhile task, but we should not be trapped by our own words. Disturbances can and should be fought, Murphy can be reduced considerably, but eliminated???

Thus, our approach should be to try and devise a mode of operation which takes into account, at any given point in time, that Murphy exists. Moreover, we must bear in mind that the struggle to reduce disturbances is not a short, one-time battle, but exactly the opposite. It is an on-going war. Thus, we should demand that our mode of operation will guide us wisely in this never-ending struggle. As a starting point, it should provide us with an on-going Pareto list: which problem should we concentrate on now, which should be solved second, and so on.

Let's face it, even when we narrow the subject of Murphy just to quality problems, how many quality problems does a plant have? Hundreds? Thousands? It's probably closer to the millions. A movement toward "total quality" can be effective only if guided by a well thought-out, always current, Pareto list.

How are we going to devise such a desirable mode of operation? As a matter of fact, the terminology we have defined so

far is almost sufficient to force us in the right direction. We have
to be both very attuned to this new terminology, and at the
same time, careful not to be held back by our inertia; inertia
that stems from old habits and new (albeit not too well-
founded) enthusiastic movements.

BUFFERS. This word alone, which was repeated so many
times in the last two chapters, indicates that our approach rec-
ognizes the existence of disturbances. But are we trying to
buffer every single task? Certainly not! The term BUFFER-
ORIGIN shows clearly that we are very selective in what we
are trying to protect. Actually we have chosen a very pragmatic
approach.

What is one of the most popular ways to describe Murphy?
What is the chance that a piece of bread will fall butter-side-
down? It's directly proportional to the price of the carpet. Are
we trying to protect all our carpets? No. Many of them can be
cleaned without any trouble—the non-constraints.

Putting jokes aside, what is the fundamental approach inherent in the terminology of BUFFERS and BUFFER-ORIGIN?
From one side, we definitely recognize the existence of Murphy,
otherwise there is no need for buffers. At the same time the
term buffer-origin reveals that we are very miserly in permitting
buffers. In other words, we are very well aware that protection
has its price; inflating inventory is also damaging. Thus we elect
to buffer only if otherwise something more important would be
lost—throughput.

This approach leads us to try and reduce, even further, the
price paid for protection. If you recall, determining the length
of the time buffers is a judgment call. How do we verify if the
length that we chose really represents the trade-off that we had
in mind? There must be some mechanism by which we can
check if we have exposed ourselves by choosing too short a
buffer, or rather than being, as we should, slightly paranoid, we
actually are hysterical.

The way the probabilistic nature of lead-time was explained
clearly indicates the technique that we should use. What was
demonstrated by Figure 3? Let's view this graph again. We de-

termined the length of the time buffer in expectation that a certain predetermined percent of the tasks will actually be at the buffer-origin at or before the required time, of course assuming they were released a buffer time ahead of the needed consumption date. What we should do now is check the real situation.

If we follow the release dates, and if our estimation of the level of disturbances is roughly correct, we should find what we expect. But if we find in the buffer-origin a larger percent of the tasks than we expected, this is a clear indication that we overestimated the length of the buffer, and in the future it should be reduced. If the opposite occurs, a larger percent than expected do not reach the buffer-origin, even at the expected consumption dates, we should increase the buffer's length. Yes, we do not like to do it, but as long as Murphy is as active in our organization as is indicated by the delays, that's the price that we have to pay to protect throughput. This brings us directly to the next issue.

How can we reduce the price of protection? Everyone who has spent some time in a company knows that a task's lead-time is a very flexible entity. It usually takes a week to complete a certain task, but if it is urgent and we give it personal attention, we can expedite it through the operations in less than a day. Of course, if we try to expedite everything, we just create havoc. But can we use expediting selectively, in order to shrink the length of the buffers?

The answer is, not surprisingly, "Yes"; we can use expediting very effectively to reduce the overall lead-time. To see how it can be done systematically let's re-examine Figure 3, the graph that displays the probabilities of a task's lead-time. To properly protect the constraints, we have to choose time buffers of a sufficient length to guarantee a high probability of the tasks arriving on time at the buffer-origin. Figure 3 clearly displays the very gradual nature of increasing probabilities at this high-percent range. To increase probability from 90% to about 98%, we need to almost double the length of the time buffer.

Let's concentrate on those tasks that have already crossed the

90% *probability* of arriving at the buffer-origin. Out of those, the ones that didn't arrive yet, let's give them a hand, let's expedite them.

This very gradual increase is the property that invites the use of expediting. Suppose we decide to take an active role in the process—rather than just launching tasks a time buffer before their scheduled consumption, we can also expedite on a selective basis. Let's concentrate on the tasks that have already crossed the 90% probability of arriving at the buffer-origin. The ones, out of those, that haven't arrived yet, let's give them a hand—let's expedite. As we said before, expediting a task considerably shrinks its lead-time. Thus, tasks that are expedited will not require the additional very long time to arrive at the buffer-origin; instead they will arrive within a relatively short time.

By expediting, we tampered with the end of the graph, making it much steeper. This mode of operation will require a relatively short time buffer to guarantee a high probability of the tasks' arrival. How much expediting will we have to do? If we stick to the quite arbitrary numbers that we have used, we'll have to expedite about 10% of the tasks, a manageable effort. Using this mode of operation, we should refer to the time interval where we use expediting as the EXPEDITING ZONE.

Of course, once again we face a trade-off. If we want to expedite fewer tasks, we will have to start expediting at a later point in time, and thus we'll have to use a longer buffer. It is a trade-off between inventory and operating expense. Bear in mind that switching to this mode of operation will drastically reduce the managerial efforts that are required today to deal with "unplanned fires." The managerial resources that are needed to deal with the "planned expediting" are usually readily available and thus no real trade-off occurs. In most cases it is simply a net reduction in the price paid for throughput protection.

How can we reduce that price even further? Until someone comes up with a really bright idea, it seems that we don't have any choice but to attack Murphy head-on. But wait, let's not continue to do it by the shotgun method. Too often in the past we have wasted our time and effort in attacking the problem we knew how to solve, just to find out that we hadn't even started to deal with the problems that we should have solved. Somehow, since we have succeeded in concentrating the protection where it is really needed, there must also be a way to concentrate our efforts to reduce the need for protection.

Maybe if we just continue to persist, we will find a way to pinpoint the problems that we should solve. We are already making the effort to monitor the buffer-origin to control the length of the buffer. It is at this point that the accumulated impact of all disturbances appears. Thus, it stands to reason that there must be a way to utilize these same efforts as a springboard for our attack on Murphy.

23. *Directing the efforts to improve local processes*

We have already noticed that if we want to reduce the price paid for protection we have to concentrate on the tasks that will arrive latest to the buffer-origin. To bring even earlier a task that will arrive ahead of time anyhow, does not help one bit to improve overall performance. We have dealt with the late tasks on an individual basis; maybe we can do much more if we deal with the more common causes for their delayed arrival.

Let's examine this interesting idea: to use the efforts done on the basis of the individual task in order to determine the more general causes for their delays. To expedite tasks, what are the sequence of actions we must take? We first determine which tasks were supposed to be in the buffer-origin, where "supposed to be" means a higher probability than, let's say, 90%. Then we check if they are actually at the buffer-origin. For the tasks that we don't find there, we start the expediting process.

The first action in expediting is to find where the delayed task is stuck. Once we find it, we take action to move it forward right away. But now let's add just one tiny thing; let's register where (in front of which resource) we found the delayed task. Repeating this for every expedited task will result in a list of resources, some of which will appear many times on the list. What is the real meaning of this list?

Suppose that there is a problem at one work center; it is more than likely that this problem will affect most, if not all, the tasks done by that resource. Moreover, if one problem at one resource affects all tasks, and another problem at another resource affects just one task, which problem is more important to deal with? This line of reasoning, acknowledging that many end problems have a common cause, leads to the recognition that the resources that appear frequently on our list do not appear there because of some statistical fluke.

A resource appears frequently because the it contains the cause of a problem common to many tasks. It might be a defective process, it might be an unreliable set-up, it might be lack of sufficient protective capacity, or it might be that the resource is simply managed very poorly. In any event, if we deal with the core problems at the resource level, rather than at the task level, we won't have to expedite repeatedly. We'll eliminate—to some extent—the reasons for expediting. Doing just that, guiding our TQM and JIT process improvement efforts by that problematic resource list, enables us gradually but consistently to shrink the length of the time buffers.

Does it mean that the length of the time buffers will always shrink? Not necessarily. Sometimes (and due to the reduction of lead times, most likely) throughput will go up. The throughput increase will lead to an increase in production loads that will eat into the available capacity for protection and thus, in order to compensate, will necessitate the increase in the time buffer's length. If done properly—with the attention always on the goal of making more money—this process will lead to controlled oscillations in the inventory levels.

It might behoove us to expand our efforts so that our problematic resource list will be more reliable. Let's remember that the time to find a core problem is usually much shorter than the time and efforts to eliminate that problem. So we should not be satisfied with the data that we gather as a side benefit only through our efforts to expedite, but we should expand our tracking efforts to cover tasks that we don't yet intend to expedite, tasks that still have ample time, but which have not arrived yet at the buffer-origin, even though there was quite a high probability that they would have arrived. To contain our efforts at a reasonable level, let's assume that we will track (but not yet expedite) every task for which the probability of its arrival to the buffer-origin has passed the 60 percent level. The resource where the task is found will be added to the list generated by our expediting efforts.

This expansion in tracking efforts will probably not only enrich the statistic, it will improve it. You see, for many tasks, if we start to track only at a very late point in time (when the probability of their arrival has already passed 90 percent) we may not find them at the resource that caused the delay. Maybe by that late time they have already passed the problematic resource, and thus problematic resources which are at the beginning of the process will rarely be caught by the expediting efforts.

In any event, starting tracking where delayed (and not just urgent) tasks are stuck will considerably improve our statistic. We should not take it too far and start tracking every task immediately after it's released; more is not always better. Starting to track immediately will not only more than double our efforts, but will also lead to a diffusion of the validity of the resulting list.

To summarize, managing the buffers provides us with several benefits. It enables us to better determine the required length in accordance with the level of existing disturbances—"quantifying the noise." It enables us systematically and methodically to expedite tasks to shrink the overall lead-time. Then, tracking the locations where the delayed tasks are found and prioritizing according to the number of times each resource appears on that list (probably with an appropriate weighting factor) provides us with the desired Pareto list, the list that should guide our "productivity improvements" efforts. But there is another, probably even more important, benefit.

What we have to bear in mind is that when we come to deal with a problematic resource, a resource that appears quite frequently on the list, we might find that its processes are in superb condition. This resource appears on our list not because of a process problem, but because it does not have enough protective capacity. Thus, buffer management provides us with the only known mechanism to estimate the required protective capacity of our resources.

QUANTIFYING MURPHY IS QUANTIFYING THE BUFFER'S LENGTH AND THE AMOUNT OF REQUIRED PROTECTIVE CAPACITY.

One word of caution is required at this point. Everything that we said so far can easily be done manually—except maybe for the extensive tracking efforts that probably should be done through a more rigorous resource report on actual transactions. But one other important issue probably cannot be fully dealt with manually. This is the subject of overcoming the need for the fluctuating portion of protective capacity by adjusting the length of the time buffers. Let's clarify this delicate subject.

When dealing with the issue of protective capacity, we have to remind ourselves that one of the major reasons for the tasks' lead time is "non-instant availability" of resources. Another side of the same coin is that fluctuations in the product mix can significantly affect the need for protective capacity, and thus a resource can appear frequently on our tracking list, due to those fluctuations. What we should remind ourselves is that this is not a problem caused by protecting the constraints, it is just clearly revealed by our systematic mode of operation. But now, maybe we should clarify why we call it a problem. It is a problem due to the fact that the span of flexible additional capacity is quite limited, usually limited to the amount of overtime available. Today we actually deal with it by adding more permanent capacity, even though this additional capacity is, by definition, useful only part of the time. We actually are forced to add excess capacity.

At first sight it seems as if we are stuck with the stochastic nature of our environment, and this is actually the case, as far as manual efforts are concerned. But there is a way out, provided that we are armed with the tremendous patience of a computer to perform voluminous calculations without being bored to death.

The way to overcome the need to add permanent capacity to cope with frequent changes in product mix stems directly from the trade-off that exists between protective capacity and length of the buffer times. But this will necessitate scheduling according to "dynamic buffering," and thus it is better to postpone the entire subject to the stage when we deal with the SCHEDULE block.

Re-examining what we have said in this chapter, it looks as if we set out to achieve one thing and actually accomplished much more. Maybe it will behoove us to continue and push a little bit more in the same direction. We were set to "quantify Murphy"; this was accomplished through the mechanism of monitoring the length of the time buffers. But we achieved more; we found a systematic mechanism to monitor the expediting efforts—not when damage had already occurred, not in a fire-fighting mode, but in a constructive way, in a way that does not aim at a specific urgent task, but which is geared to reducing the overall lead-time of all tasks. We actually achieved something that we might start to refer to as CONTROL.

Tracking the locations that are holding the delayed tasks gives us a mechanism to construct a Pareto list, both to guide our local improvement efforts and to quantify the amount of protective capacity needed per resource. As we hinted earlier, since we are now talking about tracking a considerable number of delayed tasks, this last step can be done more effectively by reporting on transactions, rather than through the more cumbersome method of tracking along the task explosion.

Reporting transactions brings the entire subject even closer to the arena of control and, at the same time, raises the disturbing, well-known issue of transaction accuracy—or shall we say transaction inaccuracy! This inaccuracy generally impairs the usefulness of data reported through transactions, but maybe we can catch a few birds with one single effort. Can we significantly improve the accuracy and timing of the reported transactions and, at the same time, answer another still open managerial question?

Let's face it, the way to improve substantially the timing and accuracy of reported transactions is to somehow make it the prime interest of the people who are supposed to report. What is the top priority of a person if not their own measurements? We are already at this level, seeking data on the steps of each individual task's progress. Why don't we take one additional small step and try to figure out how to transform this effort into the answer for the long-standing problem of local performance measurements?

Let's not forget that the question of how to measure, objectively and constructively, past local performance is one of the most burning managerial questions. If we succeed in satisfactorily answering this question, we can justifiably call this portion of our information-system "CONTROL."

24. *Local performance measurements*

Where are we headed? To the fact that in addition to instituting **BUFFER MANAGEMENT**, and on top of focusing our efforts on improving physical processes, we must institute adequate local performance measurements—measurements that by their mere existence will induce the areas measured to do what is right for the company as a whole. In order to profit from the power of the most potent force in the company—human intuition—we need to introduce a much better performance measurement system. Measuring local performance by efficiencies and variances simply drives our work force to do exactly the opposite of what we want them to do.

The need for better local performance measurements is very well known today. Unfortunately some are trying to answer this burning need with "non-financial measurements," things like defected parts per million or percent of orders not shipped on time. As we said before, as long as the goal of the company is to make money, and as long as measurements are the judge of our performance in pursuit of the goal, the units of measurement must include—by definition—the unit of money, the dollar sign. We have to dig deeper to expose the proper way to set the local measurements; we must do it. Let's remember, the issue of measurements is probably the single most sensitive issue in an organization:

144

TELL ME HOW YOU MEASURE ME AND I WILL TELL YOU HOW I WILL BEHAVE.

I don't hesitate to call performance measurement "control." I'm aware of the negative associations this word carries, because of distorted systems that are all too commonplace; nevertheless, measurements are control, self-control as much as system control.

Let's emphasize it again, because the word *control* is one of the most abused words. For example, what do we refer to when we use the term "inventory control"? The ability to know where the inventory resides. This is not control at all, this is just the ability to assemble data. For me and probably for you, control means to know where things are versus where they should be, and who is responsible for any deviation. And not in a case-by-case sporadic manner, but via a procedure that continuously attaches a numeric value to each one of the areas responsible for execution.

This is the only way we can give people the very much needed feedback about the end results of their actions. It is even more important in companies where many people are involved in the entire process, and the end result often happens in some remote department. But this way of approaching the issue of local performance measurements exposes a very interesting angle. Local performance measurements should not judge the end result, rather they should judge only the impact the local area being measured has on the end result. Local performance measurements should judge the quality of the execution of a plan, and this judgment must be totally separate from judging the plan itself.

This is especially important in our organizations, where the level in charge of execution often has very little, or even nothing, to do with setting the plan itself. If we are not careful to separate the judgment of the execution from the judgment of the plan, we might reward a department for superb performance, when actually its performance was very poor, but the plan was good enough to cover for the poor performance. Or even worse, we might condemn a department whose performance was superb, when the problems actually lie in the original plan.

These warnings bring us directly to the conclusion that when we properly judge local performance, we are actually judging deviations, deviations in the execution of a predetermined, given plan. The quality of the plan itself should be judged by the measurements that we are using all along, throughput, inventory, and operating expense. But what are the proper measures of deviation?

The first thing to recognize is that deviations from plan can happen in two different ways. The most straightforward type of deviation is "NOT DOING WHAT WAS SUPPOSED TO BE DONE." This type of deviation, which today rightfully gets almost all the attention, mainly impacts only one of the measurements. If we don't do what we are supposed to do, throughput will decrease. But there is a second type of deviation. Yes, you are right, it is "DOING WHAT WAS NOT SUPPOSED TO BE DONE." On which measurement will this type of deviation have an adverse impact? Of course, on inventory.

How can we systematically convert these obvious observations into a sound, well-defined set of measurements? Maybe we should first clarify to ourselves what unit of measure we are dealing with here. DEVIATIONS are definitely a type of liability; no one will call deviations assets, that's for sure. What is the unit of measure of a liability? Is there a generic unit at all? Let's try to find out. Take a clear example of a liability, a bank loan. This is definitely a liability. What is the unit of measure of a loan? What unit do we use to measure the damage of that liability?

When we take a loan from a bank the damage that we incur (the interest that we have to pay) is not a function merely of the amount of dollars that we borrow. We are also asked how long are we going to hold the loan. The absolute amount of money that we have to pay as interest is a function of the multiplication of the dollars that we borrow, times the length of the period that we are holding the loan. The unit of measure of a loan is DOLLARS times DAYS, or in short, DOLLAR-DAYS. Could it be that every time we deal generically with liabilities, and particularly with deviations, the appropriate unit of measure is DOLLAR-DAYS?

To examine this wild speculation, let's start by considering the entire plant as the local unit whose execution we wish to measure. On the plant level, what are the end results of deviations of the first type, not doing what was supposed to be done? The answer is obvious: the result will be not shipping on time. What is a proper measure for missed shipments?

Since in a regular company the orders vary considerably in dollar value and so do the individual products' selling prices, we can not possibly use, as a unit of measure, number of orders or number of units not shipped on time (even though, surprisingly enough, percents based on those units are in very common use). Moreover, it stands to reason that we should take somehow into account the number of days by which the order is already late. Missing an order by one single day can not be treated in the same way as missing the same order by a whole month.

A logical way to measure missed due-dates is the following: for each past-due order we should multiply the dollar amount of its selling value by the number of days the order is already late. Summing the multiplications for all late orders will give us a fair measure of the magnitude of the plant deviation from its obligation to ship orders on time. Not too surprisingly, the unit of measure comes out to be DOLLAR-DAYS, where the dollars reflect the selling prices and the days reflect the periods by which the orders are late.

Can we use the same basic technique for quantifying first-type deviations of sub-sections of an organization, sub-sections like departments or even individual resources? I don't see any reason why not.

On a department level, what will we use for the amount of dollars? There is no reason not to continue using the selling price of the final order. At the end, it is the order that, due to this department deviation, we are probably not going to ship on time. Yes, this department is holding just one part, but what are the real ramifications? What is the resulting potential damage to the company? It's not the price of that single part, it is the delay in collecting the money for the entire order.

What if it turns out that two different departments are holding back the same order, each by being late on a different task? Why don't we use, for each department, the entire selling price of the order? We don't have to share blame, we are trying to signal to each department what damage is going to be incurred to the company due to the department deviations. Let's remember, we are not going to ship due to the deviations of each department separately. If just one of those departments will not catch up, we still are not going to ship on time. Besides, we don't have any intention of summing up all the departments' deviations in order to arrive at a measure of the company as a whole. Thus, no distortion is going to be introduced by using the entire order's selling price for each department that is holding back this same order.

What are we going to use as a reference point for days—from what date are we going to consider a department as delaying a task? Somehow it doesn't feel right to wait until the order due-date, it looks like doing so is taking a too big a risk; remember, since local performance measurements are based on deviations, it should signal the local area measured, when something is going astray. If we start to signal with red flags only at that late date, the damage is already guaranteed. At that point in time, the only thing left to do is to try to minimize the damage. This does not seem to go hand in hand with our latest awakening that we should supply one hundred percent delivery on time. What should we choose as a starting point to signal (and thus to quantify and start accumulation of) deviations?

Perhaps a reasonable choice would be to start signaling when the deviation of a department has already triggered a corrective action of the organization. We have defined such points in time. Remember the expediting zone? Let's review the meaning of that zone. Sometimes an action by the organization is triggered due to a deviation in a local department. This occurs whenever a task does not arrive at its buffer-origin even though enough time had elapsed since its release, enough time to cause us, in quite high probability (let's say over 90 percent), to expect the task's arrival. Thus, we might start to count the days from the point in time when the task penetrated into the expediting zone, rather than from the order due-date. This will give us time to correct the situation before the damage to the entire company is *fait accompli.*

Maybe this will not be enough. Maybe we should start to count even earlier. We can say that an action of the organization (as compared to an action of a department) had actually been triggered long before the expediting efforts started. It began when, due to deviations, we started to track the situation of the task. Shouldn't we start to count the days from that point? Maybe.

So, we are going to multiply the selling price of the order by the number of days that have passed since a corrective action by the organization had to start. What are we going to do with the resulting number? To whom are we going to assign it?—to the one who caused the task to be delayed. How are we going to find out who really caused it—by opening an investigation agency? It will have to be much larger than the FBI, not to mention the type of argumentative atmosphere that we would force into the organization by such an action. Remember, the most sensitive issue in an organization is the individual's measurements of performance.

What do you think of the bold suggestion of assigning the responsibility, the resulting dollar-days, to the department where the task is stuck right now? Assigning it based on the current events, without considering at all which department actually caused the deviation? Looks unfair. It might be that the delayed task has just now, just a minute ago, arrived in this department, and now we're going to put all the load of the resulting dollar-days on the shoulders of someone who clearly didn't have anything to do with the delay!

Maybe at first sight this straightforward suggestion looks unfair, but wait—what are we actually trying to accomplish? Let's
not forget what we set out to do. We are trying to measure local
performance. For what purpose? In order to motivate the local
entities to do what is good for the company as a whole. Examined from this perspective, what do you think will be the
response of a department that just now was loaded with a late
task carrying considerable dollar-days with it? We all know
what the reaction will be, of course after heartily cursing the
department that originated the entire mess.

This department, now holding the late task, will take any
possible action to get rid of the "penalty" by delivering that late
task to the next department as fast as they possibly can. Moving
the task to the next department will move the dollar-days penalty with it. If for any reason no action is taken, the penalty is
bound to grow rapidly. Remember, with every passing day, the
dollar-days penalty grows. We actually gain the exact actions
that we hoped for; a late task will be expedited from one department to the other like a hot potato. The measurement itself is
triggering self-expediting.

What about the fact that doing it is simply unfair? What
about the resulting social ramifications? When we examine the
measurement along the time axis as we should, rather than at a
single point in time, we find that this brute force technique is
actually a very fair measurement. Let's view for example, the
following three graphs that represent the THROUGHPUT
DOLLAR-DAYS measurement as a function of time, for three
different departments.

What can we learn about the department whose results are
displayed in Figure 4? The spikes tell the entire story. This
department is certainly not the source of the deviations. It is a
receiving department that does an excellent job of quickly expediting the late tasks to the next department. The end result is
very good performance, the dollar-days average is very low.

The second department displays (in Figure 5) quite a different story. It's definitely not the origin of the deviations; when

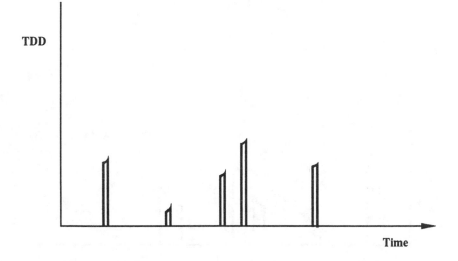

4   Throughput-Dollar-Days of a particular department as a function of time.

the tasks arrive they are already late. However, the way it deals with the late tasks is very sloppy; late tasks are allowed to stay quite a long time in the department, adding to the urgency. Of course, as a result we witness a growth in the dollar-days.

The third department is definitely the source of the deviations. Figure 6 clearly displays the growth of dollar-days, from zero value until the task is finally moved out of that department. The dollar-days average is the highest of all the departments, as it should be. Now that we have examined these three representative patterns, are you still of the opinion that attributing the dollar-days to the department where the task currently resides is in any way unfair?

As you no doubt already noticed, this measurement is perfectly applicable to every department in our organization, be it engineering, dispatching, or invoicing. The key question is always the same: right now, who is holding up the progress of the order? For example, it's not hard to imagine that under this measurement an engineering department will not feel relaxed if

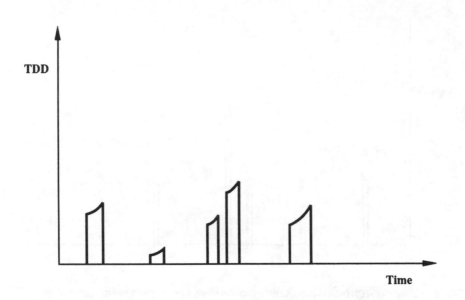

5   *Throughput-Dollar-Days of another department as a function of time.*

even one single drawing out of hundreds is not supplied to production for the manufacturing of a large system.

But another disturbing thought starts to creep in. Wouldn't this type of measurement encourage sloppy work? Won't a department, under the mounting pressure of dollar-days, choose the easy way out by delivering to downstream departments a task that is not done properly? Delivering half-baked work just to pass the ball, just to shift the "blame" onto somebody else's shoulders? If that's the case, everything that we've gained by inducing self-expediting will just create a situation that we have no desire to face.

Let's examine it calmly. Suppose that a poor-quality job has been delivered by a department. This poor quality is bound to be revealed one day, either by a downstream operation or through a complaint from a very unhappy customer. If that's the case, let's assign the corresponding dollar-days to the quality-control department. Yes, to the quality-control department.

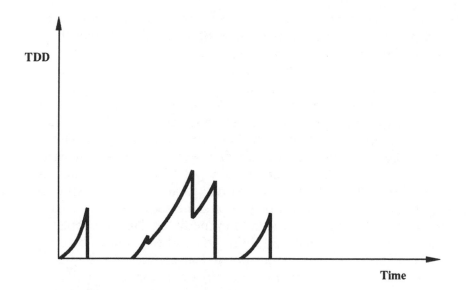

6   *Throughput-Dollar-Days of still another department as a function of time.*

I hope that by now Statistical Process Control (SPC) is extensively used in your company. While this technique is very helpful in determining when a particular part's quality is bad, its real power is its ability to determine the core reason for the poor quality, to pin down the process, and certainly the department, that produced the defect. The minute that this is done, the dollar-days are re-assigned to the department that caused the quality problem.

We cannot expect that this department will be too happy to be haunted by such a sin from the past. Remember, by now we are probably talking about a very late order (especially in the case of a client return); the number of days are considerable and so is the resulting dollar-days penalty. There is no doubt that any department would prefer to check quality many times before the task leaves the department's borders. Any quality problem revealed by downstream operations will cause the sloppy department much bigger headaches. Amazing. We were afraid that this measurement would lead to poor quality; as it turns out it leads directly to the mode of operation cherished by TQM: QUALITY AT THE SOURCE.

What about the quality-control department? Why do they have to suffer in the meantime? Let's stop using this negative terminology—blame, suffer. . . . What we are trying to do is to send the appropriate signals, so that people will know what to concentrate on in order to help the company as a whole. Take the case that we just raised, the quality-control department—what is really their primary job? To declare parts as defective? That's all? Or even worse, to sit on parts, trying to figure out whether or not they should be scrapped, and meanwhile nobody knows if we should immediately launch a replacement part or if the one held up in QC will turn out to be OK?

Their actual job is to pin down the source of the quality problem, so that the appropriate resources can take action to eliminate the problem once and for all. It looks as if the assignment of those dollar-days that resulted from quality problems to the quality-control department not only drives them to do their really important job, but also provides them with the needed Pareto list.

Look where are we now. It's apparent that we haven't finished exploring all the ramifications of using this interesting idea of THROUGHPUT DOLLAR-DAYS. We still have to deal with the second type of deviations, the ones that lead to inflating inventory, and we also need to take on the local measurement that relates to the third element, to operating expense. These deviations have to be controlled as well. What are we going to do? This chapter is already the longest in the book!

It looks as if we are starting to fall into the trap that we have tried to warn against: losing sight of what we are trying to accomplish. Let's not forget that we are trying to devise the composition and structure of an INFORMATION SYSTEM. At this rate, we'll never get there, so let's go back to our guidelines: stick to the conceptual information system's structure, and whenever it requires opening a new Pandora's Box, restrain ourselves from being totally absorbed in those interesting new topics. In our context we must provide just the guidelines and not a complete in-depth analysis.

So, for the one who wants to inquire more into the subject of local performance measurement, we can only say that a little bit more is written in the *Theory of Constraints Journal,* volume 1, Number 3.

We must paddle on.

25. *An Information System must be composed of Scheduling, Control and What-If modules*

Since we have dealt with so many subjects, it might be time to find out where we stand. We decided to cut through the existing diffusion between data and information by defining our own understanding of these words. Data for us is "every string of characters that describes anything about reality." We choose to call information "the answer to the question asked." Those elements of the data that are required in order to derive the needed information we simply call "required data."

As a result of these definitions we face situations where information is not readily available, but must be deduced from the required data. These situations forced us to realize that the deduction process is not something external to an information system, but for many types of information, the decision process itself must be an integral part of the information system.

Due to this realization, and in recognition of the currently available systems, we decided to refer to systems that supply readily available information as "data systems," and to reserve the name "information system" for systems that supply information that cannot be achieved unless through a decision process.

When we examined several managerial questions, we could

156

not escape from the realization that information is sometimes built in a hierarchical structure, where what is required data to one level is information to another level. Moreover, we encountered very important questions where the required data itself is not readily available, but must be deduced through the use of a decision process. Those cases led us to the understanding that a comprehensive information system must also be built in a hierarchical structure.

For industrial information systems, it is quite clear that at the top of the information pyramid we must answer managerial questions that are geared mainly to elevate constraints or prevent the unnecessary creation of new constraints. Belonging to this level are questions relating to investment justification, make/buy decisions, purchasing-type questions, and of course product design and sales/marketing dilemmas. We decided to refer to this upper-level portion of the information system as the WHAT IF stage.

It turned out that in order to be able even to start answering such questions, we first have to be immersed in generating the required data, data elements that by themselves are not readily available and are actually the answer for two other types of managerial questions.

The most fundamental element turns out to be the identification of the current system's constraints. Our analysis clearly showed that in order even to identify the current constraints (not to mention the need to identify the resulting constraints stemming from the evaluated WHAT IF alternative), we don't have any choice but to solve the long open question of how to schedule the operations of a company. Thus, the most basic stage of an information system is the SCHEDULE stage.

We decided to postpone the detailed discussion of how to reliably schedule an operation to the later portion of this discussion and to dive into the clarification of the other type of required data, the type of data that revolves around the quantification of disturbances accruing in the organization. Since this subject is relatively virgin territory, we had to spend considerable time clarifying the appropriate basic terminology. During this process we became more and more convinced that this stage of the information system is actually dealing with managerial questions revolving around the subject of CONTROL.

The CONTROL stage contains the ability to quantify Murphy, which is essential for getting a handle on the magnitude of trade-off between inventory and protective capacity, and thus for being able to answer, quite reliably, any WHAT IF question. Moreover, this same mechanism is needed in order to supply different, but still necessary, types of information. One is the answer to the question of where to concentrate our efforts to reduce Murphy—where to focus our efforts to improve processing. The second is the badly needed local performance measurements.

So far, we have established that the information system needs to be comprised of three stages or blocks: the WHAT IF, the SCHEDULE, and the CONTROL blocks. We have also established that the WHAT IF block cannot possibly be done before the other two blocks are operational, simply because the information supplied by these two blocks is needed as data for the WHAT IF block. But what is the relationship between the SCHEDULE and CONTROL blocks? Are they totally independent of each other, or is one a prerequisite for the other?

Even a cursory examination reveals that the CONTROL block cannot be used before the SCHEDULE block is operational. What did we say is the meaning of control?—to know where things are versus where they SHOULD HAVE BEEN. We should control deviations from a predetermined plan; thus scheduling—planning—must be established before CONTROL can start. But let's examine conceptually what it is that we try to control in more detail, so that we will be able to expose the requirements that the SCHEDULE block must meet.

Deviations that impact throughput and deviations that impact inventory are deviations from realistic plans. This means that our plan—schedule—must already provide for the existence of Murphy, otherwise it cannot be a realistic plan. It is mandatory that the SCHEDULE block provide a plan according to some predetermined estimation of the level of Murphy existing in the plant. Only in this way can the SCHEDULE module provide realistic schedules and CONTROL, striving to reduce Murphy's impact, have real-life meaning.

Thus the SCHEDULE stage must be fed with rough estimates of the time buffers and of the required levels of protective capacity, estimates that will be refined later by the CONTROL stage. Trying to use the WHAT IF stage before somewhat reliable levels of protective capacity have been determined through *using* the other two stages is, in my eyes, just a waste of time.

The action plan is now outlined. The information system's first stage that must be constructed is the SCHEDULE phase. The only data needed, in addition to what is now commonly used, is a rough guesstimate of the impact of the existing Murphy. Once this phase is operational, the second phase can be put in practice, the CONTROL phase. And only after they have been used for some time can we reach the information system's ultimate goal: the ability to answer our WHAT IF questions.

Now we need to start to deal with the structure of the first required phase—the SCHEDULE—but not as before. We just reached the foundation, and thus we can no longer leave subjects open, being satisfied by showing just the conceptual direction. From now on, every detail should be hammered thoroughly.

PART THREE
SCHEDULING

26. *Speeding up the process*

So now we are stuck with the unenviable task of outlining the approach to the scheduling phase. Is it going to be easy, just a boring technical task? Probably neither. Let's not forget that scheduling was the main objective of MRP; nevertheless, after thirty years of mammoth efforts, where do we stand? It is a general consensus among all practitioners that, in spite of all efforts, MRP is not a scheduler, but just a very much needed data bank.

This is not too surprising, since the throughput-based decision process was not available to the originators of MRP. That's why, as we indicated earlier, almost all additional efforts during the past thirty years have been geared toward the fruitless attempt to extend data availability. At least, now, we're going to benefit from these efforts; in devising the schedule phase we will not have to concern ourselves with the availability of most of the basic data; everyone has it captured already, in one form or another. Usually, as a matter of fact, in more than one form; it's not rare to find companies who have three different bill-of-material records for exactly the same product.

Still, it looks as if we can not escape from re-examining the way that data is currently handled by our computers. You see, our experience with MRP has taught us another, quite unpleasant, lesson. The time required to generate a schedule, even an erroneous and non-detailed one, is quite exorbitant. For small

163

plants, we usually talk about hours of computer time; and for big complicated organizations, an entire weekend is sometimes not sufficient. Is this a real concern, an essential ingredient we must deal with now, or are we just entering the trap of trying to avoid facing the need to develop a "good enough" solution by banging our heads against the wall of prematurely polishing a solution that is not yet outlined?

In other words, is the length of time required to generate a schedule a decisive factor that will totally prevent us from using the information system, or is it just a nuisance? At first sight, it looks as if the situation calls for devising a schedule—period. The fact that we would like to get it as fast as possible really doesn't matter, as long as we're going to get it eventually. But this can not possibly be the generic answer.

To prove it is simple. Just imagine that the time required to generate a schedule for one week is more than a week. If that's the situation, the method is certainly not practical. The generation time is not a nicety, it's an essential ingredient that must be considered while devising the solution. You see, there must be an upper limit on the time that the generation of the schedule will take, a limit that if crossed will definitely declare the method worthless.

Big deal, why do we waste our time on things that are obvious? Because it might be that our impatience stems from the unsubstantiated assumption that most feasible solutions to the scheduling problems will, without any additional efforts, be within the tolerable limits. Is it really the case? It definitely seems like it. We already have, from our scheduling experience, a reasonable estimate for that upper limit. We know that we can tolerate schedule generation time of many hours or even an entire weekend. . . .

So why should we be concerned with the generation time limitations? But wait, let's not rush. Our experience stems from a reality in which we related to scheduling as an end in itself, and not as a required step for something else. Is it possible, when we evaluate the schedule as a phase in a bigger process, the "what if" process, that our intuition will demand we considerably reduce the upper limit? Reduce it to the extent that the many hours required to generate a detailed schedule for a span of several weeks will be out of the question?

To clarify the situation, try to imagine that you, as a manager, are trying to decide between several available alternatives. Let's not forget that the vast majority of management questions have an impact, not only on the immediate future, but also on the medium-range horizon. Examine for example the list of questions appearing at the beginning of Chapter 17. What is the horizon of time involved in each one of them? It ranges between a few months and a few years. As we said before, to evaluate each one of the alternatives reliably, we will have to reveal the impact they will have on the system's constraints, and thus a schedule for the entire relevant time-span must be done, a detailed schedule.

If we use the traditional method, how much time will it take? Certainly many hours, probably days. If you have to spend so much time to evaluate even one alternative out of many, do you really believe that you will use that information system? The unavoidable conclusion is that we must demand from the schedule phase that it will complete a long-term detailed schedule of the entire company in less than one or two hours. This is a horrifying demand, but probably inescapable.

To drastically shrink the time required for scheduling, it looks as if there is no choice but to re-examine every time-consuming step—even the way that data is currently handled by the conventional MRP systems. To examine it critically, in order to find out where the majority of the elapsed time is absorbed. Once again, whenever we face a long-standing problem, it looks as if we don't have a choice but to dig into the hidden roots of the problem.

Why does an MRP run take so long? Computers are famous for being extremely fast. Knowing something about computers, we realize that two distinct speeds are involved in a computer— the speed at which the computer calculates, and the speed at which the computer stores and retrieves data. Both of these speeds are quite remarkable, but they are drastically different.

The speed at which the computer calculates, using what we call its Central Processing Unit (CPU) and its on-line memory, is quite outstanding. Even personal computers can multiply two large numbers in less than one millionth of a second. The computer speed is quite different when it retrieves or writes a block of data to its data storage media—disks. We call this latter mode of operation Input/Output (I/O) mode. Even when we consider the commercially available, broadly used, fastest disks, we are dealing with times which are longer than one hundredth of a second. A remarkable speed—but a snail's pace compared to the computing speed.

The way that we wrote our currently available scheduling packages definitely highlights the fact that most of the computer time is engaged in retrieving and writing data, back and forth, to the disks. Every professional will tell you, without hesitation, that MRP is "totally I/O bound." Which means, in more simple words, that the vast majority of the time is not spent on computations, but on the internal shuffling of data. Even the very small percent of the time which is declared by the computer as CPU time, tends to be, on closer examination, the CPU time that the computer had to invest to handle the data manipulation. Only a fraction of a percent of the total time that we are waiting for the computer to deliver the schedule is actually devoted to calculations.

Must it be like that, or can we do something to improve the existing situation? As it turns out the mentality that we use to code the computer is still heavily influenced by technological limitations that existed in the past—limitations that are now totally overcome, even in the smallest commonplace personal computers (PCs).

You see, less than 15 years ago, a programmer did not have a powerful computer at his command, a computer with more than one million bytes for on-line data handling (on-line memory). All of our experienced programmers, and certainly all the programming textbooks, are based on experience gained in an environment where they had to struggle with the strait jacket of not having enough memory available for their programs.

Even when the big mainframes arrived on the scene, bringing on-line memory of millions of bytes, every programmer knew that if a program needed a big chunk of that memory, the program would have to wait for many hours in the queue. Remember, those mainframes were used by many users—quite a drastic difference from our world of personal computers. Under those memory restrictions, there was no choice but to store and then retrieve intermediate values (especially when we recall that the mean time between failures was in the few hours' range).

The inertia stemming from past restrictions has masked the huge difference in the preference that a computer has versus human preferences. Suppose that you have two lists, each fifty items long. One list details the price per unit, and the other details the quantity of each item to be purchased. You would like to know the total amount of money that you will have to pay. One avenue open to you is to multiply every number on the first list with its corresponding number on the second list and total the fifty results. Or, you can just flip the page to read the final answer; it's written there. What would you prefer to do? No doubt, flip the page. But the computer won't.

For a computer "flipping a page" means to access the disk and bring from it, to the memory, a string of data. This I/O operation will take the computer a few hundredths of a second. To carry out 50 multiplications, and then sum the results, will take the computer a few millionths of a second. The computer prefers to carry out the entire calculation 1,000 times rather than to bring the final result from its disk.

Our commercially available packages are, in general, not utilizing this tremendous capability of computing power. Rather, they go back and forth to the disk to bring strings of data which could be internally recalculated much, much faster. Of course the latter method requires holding somewhat more data in on-line memory, but as we said before, the limitations on available memory have been drastically reduced. If we pay attention to this difference, between calculating speed and retrieving speed, we can shrink the total computer-run by over 1000 times.

This is basically what we need to do here, but even though we do have a lot of memory, if wasted it might still be a real limitation. Therefore we should examine the way we are going to store and manipulate the data, which will dictate the overall run times, and thus the mere feasibility of our entire information system.

27. Cleaning up some more inertia— rearranging the data structure

The most tedious and time-consuming part of scheduling is the explosion process. Explosion means to start at the order level, the external requirements, and to dive down along the product structure in order to determine the needs, both in quantity and time, at the lower levels, the assembly, component production, and purchasing levels.

Today the product structure is usually not contained as a single entity, rather, it is broken down into two separate categories, Bill Of Materials (BOM) and Routings. This separation forces the need to jump back and forth between two different segments of the data base, which naturally inflates the computer response time drastically. But think about it, both BOM and Routings are descriptions of the "journey" that material has to go through in operations, in order to be converted to something that satisfies the client's needs. So, why the need for this awkward segmentation?

It is amazing to see the response of system designers when they are confronted with the question, "Why was the product structure's file segmented into the BOM and Routing files?" Usually you will hear either a flood of technical buzz words that will leave your head spinning, or some awkward philosophical, almost metaphysical, arguments. Actually what we face here is just our old and not so good friend, inertia. Yes, there was a very practical, almost mandatory, reason for their segmentation. There was such a reason, but it doesn't exist anymore.

Let's do some archaeological digging to expose the real reason. Let's start at the beginning, in the early sixties, when the main effort to construct the conceptual design of MRP was done. At that time, the only available storage for voluminous amounts of data was magnetic tapes. On tapes, data can be stored and retrieved only in a sequential way; this technological limitation presented the designers of MRP with a phenomenal problem.

Examine the situation they faced when the product structure contained a major assembly required in different final products. See, for example, Figure 7.

Such a description, although natural, is an impossibility when the storage media is tapes. The closest approximation is to detail the assembly within the first product, and only mention it at the other products (as shown in Figure 8).

But what would have happened if they had chosen that description? Each time that one of the other products needed to be exploded, the tape would have to be rewound to get the assembly's details. You know how much time it takes to rewind a tape? Not fractions of a second anymore, but minutes—not to mention the fact that so many winds and rewinds would be needed that the tape would probably tear before the end of the run.

The other bad alternative that they faced was to detail the major assembly data for each and every product that requires it (as shown in Figure 9).

The problem is not so much the explosion that will result in the need to store so much data. The problem is revealed after the initial effort, when the stage of maintaining the data is reached. Changes occur in this major assembly. It is updated in most of the places, but not in all—some are always overlooked. It doesn't take long until the discrepancies arrive at a level where the entire system is not usable anymore.

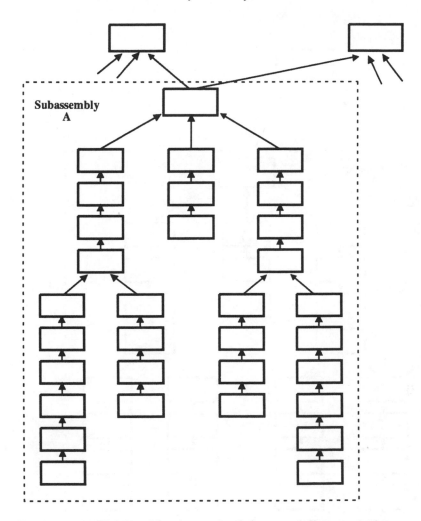

7 *A major subassembly A, required for two different products.*

Facing the devastating choice between horrible and even worse alternatives, the designers of MRP decided on a compromise. They created the concepts of BOM and Routing. Actually, what they did was to repeat only the major structural details of the assembly everywhere—what we call today BOM —and to store the vast majority of the detailed data only once

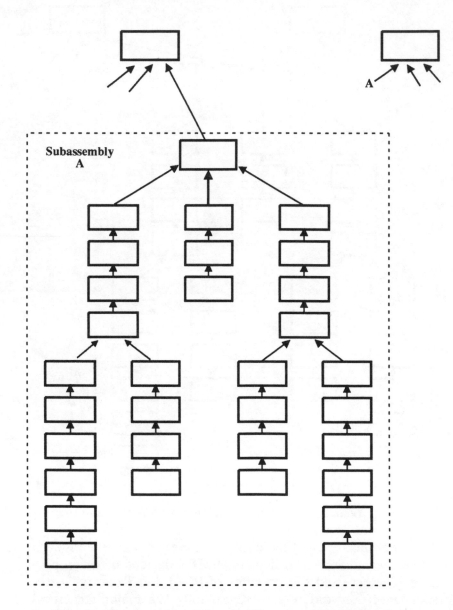

8 *The details of a major subassembly presented in full only at one product and just indicated at others.*

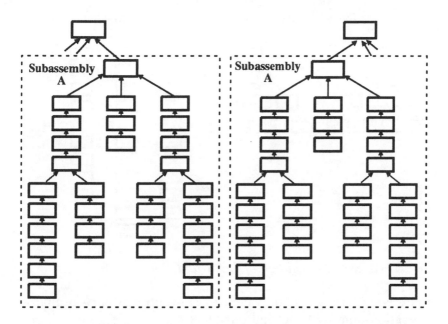

9 *A major subassembly A, presented in full at each product requiring it.*

—what we call Routing. The end result is displayed in Figure 10. Was it a perfect solution? Far from it, but it worked.

Since then, disks have replaced tapes as storage media. Disks enable direct access, rather than just sequential; by moving the head of the disk, just like playing a record, we can directly reach any point on the plate. Disks removed the technical limitation which caused the problem to begin with, but by that time it was too late. BOM and Routing were rooted to the extent that they took on a life of their own. No one dared to question this sacred segmentation.

Realizing the current capabilities of computers, we should use a product structure that does not differentiate between BOM and Routing, each entry representing a stage in the "journey." We basically are back to the most fundamental picture, the one shown in Figure 7 (see page 171). Every step in the

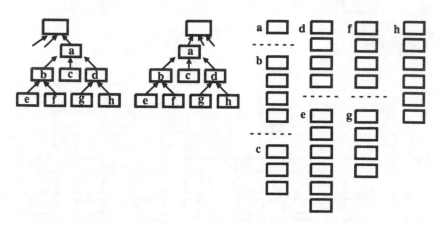

Bill of Material   **Routing**

10   The comprised solution of BOM and Routings.

material "journey" is equivalent to conventional part-number/ operation-number. A trivial change.

For a person who hasn't spent many years in an MRP environment it doesn't even look like a change, it is a natural choice. But the impact on computer execution time is quite profound. This merger between the conventional BOM and Routing drastically reduces the number of times we need to access the disks and thus speeds up the entire process by orders of magnitude. What a price we have paid because of our inertia!!

But let's not stop here, let's merge some more data files into our product structure. Today most systems are holding separately two additional files. One is usually called "stores inventory" and the other "work-in-process (WIP) inventory." Basically the stores inventory details the quantity of available completed parts, assemblies, and materials, while the WIP file contains the inventory of partially processed parts. What is the reason for this separation, which inflates, once again, the time to do the explosions?

When we consider some units which are partially processed,

from a system design point of view, we are faced with the need of coding them—of attaching a code name to these units. Actually, for this case we have two alternative choices. We can code the inventory according to the code name of the last operation that the units have completed, or we can code it according to the code name of the next operation they should go through. Both choices are equivalent. No wonder that the system's designers, in the early '60s, decided to choose according to the practice on the shop floor. Where do we hold the partially processed items? In the queue right in front of the next machine. In other words, we physically assign the WIP inventory according to the next operation it should go through. That was a natural choice.

This choice, which is so natural for partially processed parts, is totally inadequate when we are considering finished parts. Here we don't have a choice of coding the inventory according to the next operation; the next operation is assembly. Coding it according to the assembly's code name gives the false impression that all other components needed for that assembly are also available.

For finished parts the only choice is to code the stored inventory according to the last operation performed on the part. This different choice necessitates a segmentation between the two inventory files, a segmentation that didn't bother the early designers too much, since it mirrors the segmentation between BOM and Routing that was already in effect. We, who have merged the two product structure's files, will have to be more consistent. We will always name the inventory according to the last operation that it passed through. This will not only enable us to converge both inventory files into one, it will enable the convergence of the inventory data into a single field, residing in the product structure's file.

The resulting shrinkage in the number of files opens the possibility of holding the entire needed data in memory. This can be achieved only if we don't inflate the data required for scheduling with other details which don't have anything to do with it, like the address of a vendor, or the angle by which the material should be cut. Likewise, we have to be careful not to store too many intermediate computational results. If we do, it will "eat" very quickly into the available memory, and we will be forced to turn to the disks. Remember, to repeat a lengthy calculation is much faster than reaching for the disk.

Having the ability to hold all the required data in memory will enable the computer to reach for the disks only at the beginning of the scheduling run—to copy the data into memory, and then at the end—to write the schedule. Today's availability of memory, which reaches megabytes even on a PC, enables us to operate in this desirable mode. The result is, not surprisingly, a drastic cut in execution time. Scheduling of a large plant, in detail, for a horizon of many months or even years, can now be achieved, on today's powerful PCs, in considerably less than one hour.

Of course the conversion problem is starting to raise its ugly head. How are we going to convert from the existing multi-file structure to the suggested uniform "tasks-structure net"? This problem seems even more complicated when we remind ourselves that in our current files much more data elements are involved, much more than is strictly needed for the simulation of the company's future actions. Aren't those additional data elements going to turn the suggested scheme into a different, but not less complicated, nightmare?

Maybe yes, maybe no. But the real question that we have to ask ourselves is whether or not we have to convert all our data base. Do we really have to bother? We are dealing here with constructing an information system and not with trying to improve our existing data systems. In any event we already came to the conclusion that an information system is not a replacement for a data system; rather our information system should suck its required data from a data system.

Moreover, we have already agreed that the main purpose of an information system is to deal with hypothetical situations, with "what if" questions. At the same time, we are quite well aware that managers at different levels and different functions are bothered by different types of "what if" questions. Thus each manager will have to adjust the base data to create the desirable, unique "hypothetical" situations they would like to examine. The conclusion is almost unavoidable: an information system, and thus its own specific, required data, must be made available on a distributed, disseminated basis.

Should we treat our data systems in the same way? In my eyes, it's a recipe for disaster. Holding our data systems on a decentralized computer net guarantees that, with time, discrepancies in the data will start to mushroom. Try to imagine the chaos that will result when different managers, assuming that they are working on the same data base, start to make decisions which are actually based on different sets of data. No, the current heated debate between the opponents of centralized and decentralized processing actually stems from the current confusion between data systems and information systems. A data system must be centralized. Information systems, all fed from the single data bank, must be decentralized. Isn't it obvious?

This realization is also a very good guideline for the needed conversion in the data format. There is no need to restructure the existing data banks. What we have to concentrate on is the structure of the subset of data that must become available for the information system. Since almost every company is storing its data in a different format and file layout, there is no point in trying to devise a totally generic conversion package. Rather we should try to reduce to the bare minimum the portion of the programming efforts that must be tailored to the existing format of the existing data systems, making sure that this programming effort will be trivial enough to be done by any programmer. The more sophisticated portion, the portion dealing with meshing the sporadic files into a uniform net, can then be standardized through a package.

Even though finding the proper segmentation might look at first sight like a difficult problem, it's actually a no-brainer. We just have to ignore, for a moment, our burning desire to complicate things, to make them more "sophisticated," and the solution becomes obvious. Every programmer knows how to extract, from the data base, a sequential file that contains in each record just a subset of predetermined fields. As a matter of fact, for most data systems, it is a standard utility. Let's do it for each file separately, for the Bill-Of-Material file, for the Routing file, for the Inventory file, for the Work-In-Process file, for the resources availability file, for the open customer file, and for the external forecast consumption file. Now we are in a standard data structure, unrelated to the specific structure of the existing data base, and thus we can continue the more complicated part of the conversion using a standard interface.

What do we need in addition? The calendar of the organization, or several calendars for cases where different departments are following different calendars—like a division composed of sectors located in different countries. What else? Oh, some parameters like the length of the various time-buffers and estimation of the needed level of protective capacity.

But let's stop this procrastination; it's obvious that we have put the problems of execution-time and data-conversion behind us, at least on the conceptual level. It's about time to turn our attention to the real issue; how should we schedule according to the realization of the throughput world?

28. *Establishing the criteria for an acceptable schedule*

Schedule the tasks an organization should perform! Easy to say, but where do we even begin? Should we start from the clients' orders and explode down into the tasks levels? If so, which order should we pick first? The biggest in sales value? The one which represents the largest load? The one that we already suspect might be late in delivery? Or maybe we should try a totally different attack, like starting with the tasks that right now are stuck in the pipeline. Cleaning the system looks like not too bad an idea. But a tiny voice is whispering, somewhere in the background, that since we discussed the problem of limited capacity for so long, it would be best to start by sequencing the tasks of one of the most loaded resources and go from there. So many possibilities—none of them looks too promising, especially when we find that each one of them has already been tried more than once, leading to schedules that were certainly nothing to write home about.

Well, we have to start someplace. But before struggling with the question of "where to start," we'd better clarify what we are actually trying to achieve. A schedule! Isn't it clear? Not necessarily. What type of schedule are we attempting to construct? What schedule will satisfy us?

It's starting to dawn on us that the first step in devising a

179

schedule is to define the criteria that a "good" schedule must fulfill. The first criterion is very obvious: the schedule must be realistic. But wait a minute—what do we mean by that word *realistic?* Let's not be satisfied with using words with too broad a meaning, words that will not give us a firm grasp of what we actually are supposed, or not supposed, to do. What can cause a schedule to be regarded as unrealistic?

Just think about that last question, and it becomes apparent that two different things can cause us to declare a schedule as an unrealistic schedule. The first one is if we generate a schedule that our system can not possibly carry out. That might happen if the schedule ignores the inherent limitations of our system. What did we call those things that limit our system's performance? Constraints. Thus any realistic schedule must start by recognizing the system's constraints. Not an overwhelming conclusion; we already stated more than once that the first step (once the goal and measurements have been defined) is always IDENTIFY THE SYSTEM'S CONSTRAINTS.

But is it sufficient to identify the constraints in order to guarantee a realistic schedule? Not necessarily; we may run into situations where there are conflicts between the constraints. For example, a company promised deliveries beyond its resources' capability to meet the promised due-dates. When is the time to straighten out these conflicts? Are we going to let reality sort them out? This mode of operation will, no doubt, lead to some unpleasant surprises. We had better carefully examine such future conflicts and resolve them before reality resolves them by default. It is apparent that a realistic schedule should not contain any conflict between the system's constraints.

This last statement sheds new light on the process by which a schedule should be constructed. We have already come to the realization that identifying the constraints—and thus creating a schedule—will have to be carried through an iterative process, through going over and over the steps of IDENTIFY, EXPLOIT, SUBORDINATE, finding each time an additional constraint. We already stated that this process will have to go on until at the end of the SUBORDINATION step no violations are found. Now we realize that whenever an additional constraint is found we will have to check thoroughly if there are conflicts between the identified constraints.

Moreover, since those conflicts were unrecognized before (otherwise they would already have been removed), it is more than likely that the required data to resolve the conflicts is not clearly specified, that these elements of data exist mainly in the more intuitive know-how. For example, if the only way to resolve a conflict is by postponing clients' orders, the know-how of which order we can postpone without creating too big a conflict with the client is usually not documented at all. Should we, as systems designers, demand that this type of required data be fully and explicitly documented? In my eyes, this would be a totally unrealistic demand. If this turns out to be a mandatory demand, we'd better pack our bags and drop the entire subject.

So, what else is left to be done when a conflict between the constraints is revealed? The answer must be that the information system has to concentrate on revealing the conflicts, highlighting in each case the optional minimum actions that can be taken in order to remove the conflict; but unless very clear guidelines have been established, the information system must, at that point, stop and demand that the user make the decision.

This is a far-reaching conclusion. Compare it with the other scheduling methods that have been used in the last decades. To linear programming, for example, the technique that boldly presents the user with an end result where conflicts have been "resolved," ignoring the fact that a lot of the data required for a proper resolution of the conflicts has not been presented. Moreover, it doesn't even bother to highlight where the conflicts have been encountered and what assumptions have been made in resolving them. For the user, it's basically a black box that arrogantly puts a set of mathematical equations above the superior capabilities of the human brain to find amicable resolutions by simply changing the assumptions of the problem, whenever a "no way out" situation is encountered. No wonder that linear programming (or it's bigger and more "sophisticated" sister, dynamic programming) has not succeeded in finding a broad application, in spite of the fact that for no real reason it has been the cornerstone of operation research for the last twenty years.

Compare our conclusion to the scheduling method of Just-In-Time, the KANBAN system, the method that decided to off-load the entire subject of dealing with conflicts from the scheduling phase to the execution phase—almost the antithesis of linear programming. No coherent guidelines have been established to guide us in selecting the number and content of the various cards to be located between the various work centers; the full load of making the schedule work is placed on the floor personnel.

Look at the MRP method, that a priori has given up on the requirement to be realistic, as can be clearly understood by it's motto, "infinite capacity." Yes, MRP is trying to correct the situation by introducing the "closed loop" concept, a concept through which the finite capacity of the company's resources are taken into account. But even a casual examination reveals that the closed loop is an iterative process that NEVER CONVERGES. In the name of realistic procedure MRP has presented an unrealistic procedure.

It is quite apparent that this trivial demand of having realistic schedules is not trivial at all. If our information system is to be effective in answering "what if" managerial questions, we have to take the requirement of realistic schedules much more seriously than previously attempted.

Before we take a deep breath and continue on, we must remind ourselves that in calling a schedule realistic, we had two requirements in mind. One was the resolution of conflicts between the constraints. What was the second? Oh yes, the second requirement that a schedule should fulfill is that it will be immune against disruptions. This is not exactly a new requirement for us; we have dealt with it in considerable length in the previous chapters, but not as part of the schedule itself. We have dealt with this subject as part of the control. Does the subject of immunity belong to scheduling? We cannot escape the realization that it definitely belongs.

Schedule, by definition, concerns some interval of time. If the purpose of scheduling is to identify future constraints, the schedule must be definitely realistic for that future interval of time. If any perturbation, if any action of Murphy, will necessitate rescheduling, it is the best indication that the currently generated schedule is totally unrealistic for the required future time interval. Immunity seems to be a mandatory requirement for a schedule.

Have the past methods taken immunity into account? Not quite. Linear programming didn't hesitate to present "solutions" that were based on interactive constraints. That was done in spite of the fact that every sensitivity analysis (which is an integral part of linear programming) clearly indicated, in those numerous cases of interactive constraint solutions, that the resulting schedules are unstable schedules, that any disruption will totally invalidate the suggested schedules. No, even though all indications were present, we elected to ignore immunity as a valid requirement.

What about JIT and MRP? These methods were much more practical, but unfortunately not practical enough. Both methods realized that immunity against disruptions is a must for schedule; they have realized it to the extent that they both have allowed for more time to be spent for immunization than for actually carrying out the tasks themselves! Nevertheless, the resulting schedules of both methods are far from being immunized, as can be easily seen by the demand that they place on the floor personnel to resolve "surprises." The main problem stems from the fact that both methods have tried to immunize the schedule itself rather than the result of the schedule. This approach has forced them to try and protect each individual instruction, a method that defeated itself. You see, the unavoidable result of trying to protect every operation was over-extension of the lead time to fulfill the end client requirements. To overcome this problem the individual "spare time" (either represented by number of KANBAN cards or by queue and wait time) had to be trimmed to the extent that, once again, we faced unstable schedules.

What is required is immunity of the schedule to the extent that the predictions of the schedule will be realistic—the prediction about the expected performance of the organization, and the prediction about the organization's constraints.

Is that all? Have we finished outlining the criteria by which we should judge a schedule? Not yet. We still haven't mentioned the most important one. Why do we need a schedule to start with? Let's not forget what it's all about. When we are devising a schedule the target is, as always, to strive to achieve the goal. Thus the schedule, once it is realistic, must be judged by the same measurements that we usually use to judge results: throughput, inventory, and operating expense.

We have to bear in mind the measurements' scale of importance, and thus whenever we face a situation where throughput is going to be jeopardized, a situation that we can correct by increasing inventory or operating expense, we should take the appropriate corrective actions without hesitation. But here a word of caution is in place. Whenever we are increasing inventory or operating expense we have to be very careful not to clash with necessary conditions.

For example, if in order to protect throughput we should increase material inventory (by making the release earlier then otherwise needed), the information system should do it. But if in order to protect throughput we need to increase capacity, either by buying a new machine or by authorizing overtime, the information system should be much more careful—buying a new machine might violate the necessary condition of cash. Moreover, a lot of required data to make such a decision is lacking, like the delivery time of a new machine or the new capabilities that are now offered for such a technology.

Likewise, when more overtime than is already permitted is required, the information system cannot authorize the required additional overtime. We should not neglect the fact that a lot of the required data needed for making such a decision (like the willingness of the people involved to do more overtime, or their effectiveness when overtime is used too aggressively) is simply not available to the system. We should not even demand that this type of data be made available to the information system. In most cases it is much too voluminous, and usually it exists only at the intuitive level. No, in such cases our information system must just highlight the situation and leave the specific decision to the user.

In summary, an information system must generate a schedule which is first of all realistic: it must not contain any conflict between the organization's constraints, and it must be immunized against a reasonable level of disruptions. The resulting realistic schedules are judged by the usual measurements. In other words, the end performance that the schedule indicates is judged by whether or not maximum throughput has been achieved (maximum in terms of exploitation of the company's constraints). Second in importance is the level of material inventory that is going to be required as a function of time. Any material inventory should be present only in order to guarantee the throughput; otherwise it should be declared as excess inventory and the schedule should be judged accordingly.

As for operating expense, the information system is allowed to use overtime only within the parameters specified to it, and in those cases the only valid reason to use overtime is to protect the company's throughput. Any other increase in inventory (like machines or fixtures) or operating expenses (like additional personal or special overtime) must be dictated by the user, and thus, even though it must be a part of the measurements used to judge the end schedule, it shouldn't be part of judging the information system itself.

29. *Identifying the first constraints*

Now it is very obvious where our efforts to devise a schedule should start—by identifying the company's constraints. What might be a constraint? Remember, we already agreed that no policy constraints will be taken into account by our information system; policy constraints should be elevated, not exploited. What is left are the physical constraints: market constraints, resource constraints, and vendor constraints. This is still much too broad for a good starting point, so let's try to narrow it down further. How?

Should we just declare something as being a constraint so that we'll have a definite starting point? This might work under two conditions. The first condition is that at the end we will have a clear indication if our original choice was right or wrong. Remember, we are doing the scheduling mainly in order to identify all constraints. The second condition, which is definitely not less important, is that we'll be guaranteed that when it turns out that our original choice was wrong—that we actually started with a non-constraint—nevertheless, the resulting schedule will be acceptable.

Unfortunately, considering, for the purpose of scheduling, everything that we have discussed so far, it is quite clear that the above conditions are not met. It seems that the only mechanism that can point to something that was erroneously considered to be a constraint and clearly declare it as a non-constraint

186

is "buffer management." But relying on that technique means that the wrong assumption will be revealed only by watching the execution of the doubtful schedule in reality for a while. This is much too late. No, we must start with identifying something that is definitely a constraint.

Must we identify all the constraints before we can move to the next step and try to exploit them? There is no need. As we said before, identifying the constraints is an iterative process; we'll have to move through the steps of IDENTIFY, EX- PLOIT, SUBORDINATE over and over, each time adding an- other constraint to the list, until we reach the stage where at the end of subordination no violation with reality can be found. Only then will we finish.

This implies that whenever we are in doubt as to whether or not something is a constraint, it is much safer to assume that it is not. You see, if it's not a constraint, and we declare it as a constraint, we are going to be stuck with it. But if it is a real constraint, and at this stage we decide to ignore it, no harm has been done, since we'll eventually catch it in one of the following rounds. So the question is, what can we, right at the start, declare with very high probability as a constraint?

To start by picking a vendor or even a specific material as a constraint is apparently much too risky. A material can be iden- tified as a constraint only when we compare its current and future availability to the timing and quantities of the needed consumption. This implies having, at the start, detailed knowl- edge of what we are actually seeking to generate by this process —the schedule. No, to decide to start with a vendor constraint is a very poor choice, especially when we recall many, many situations in which no vendor constraint existed.

Can we start with a resource constraint? Maybe, but let's remember that most resource constraints that we face in reality are not bottlenecks, but resources that do not have sufficient protective capacity. The "trademark" of a resource constraint that does not have enough protective capacity is that such a resource, even though it has on average enough capacity, can- not handle its peaks of load. Thus we can identify it only through examining the details of the requirement as a function of time. Once again, we face a situation where, in order to identify such a constraint, first we need the schedule itself. No, we cannot build a general procedure based on the unrealistic assumption that in any situation there is at least one resource which does not have enough capacity to satisfy the market demand.

Well, our floundering did get us somewhere; the only choice left is to start from market constraints—the client orders. But before we plunge on, we'd better check if it is correct to assume, with high probability, that client orders can always be taken as constraints. Just to say there is no other alternative left is to assume that we didn't ignore any possibility in our analysis. This is definitely not just an arrogant assumption; it is also a very dangerous one.

So let's ignore the fact that we have already disqualified all other known possibilities, and let's concentrate on examining whether or not we can safely assume that client orders are always a constraint of our organization. (By the way, this will highlight the fact that we should change our attitude toward constraints; if client orders are constraints, constraints are not necessarily a bad thing.)

If there are no internal constraints in our organization, then the market demands are the constraints (let's ignore, for the moment, the possibility of vendor constraint). If we have internally everything in excess, then the only thing that limits us from making more money is the market demand. What about the cases where we do have internal capacity constraints? Is it safe to assume in these cases that the market is still a constraint (remember, we assumed no policy constraints for the purpose of our information system)? Let's distinguish between two cases, where we do have bottlenecks, and where we have only capacity constraints due to lack of sufficient protective capacity. It will be easier to deal with the latter case, so let's start with it.

The amount of needed protective capacity a resource has to have is a function of the length of the time buffer. If no due-date is specified (implicitly or explicitly), the length of the time buffer is not limited and therefore there is no need for any protective capacity. Thus, whenever we deal with a case where a resource constraint exists due to lack of sufficient protective capacity we, by definition, deal with a case where the market demands are the prime constraint.

What is left to examine is the case of a bottleneck, a resource that does not have sufficient available capacity to strictly satisfy the demand (the following analysis of the bottleneck case is exactly identical to the analysis required for the case of a vendor or specific material constraint, and thus it will not be detailed separately). Our small "P and Q" quiz taught us that when a bottleneck is participating in the fulfillment of more than one product, then market demands for all the products except for one are, nevertheless, constraints of the system. Moreover, unlike the quiz, we usually have due-dates—we have to supply to our client no later than a specified date. In such a case the specific order will still be a constraint.

It turns out that the only case in which we cannot take the market as a constraint is when we don't have to commit delivery dates to the clients. We have a resource constraint producing just one product, and every unit that we offer is immediately grabbed by the market. Let's face it, that case is very rare, so if we do have client's orders with specified dates attached, it is safe to assume the client's orders are constraints.

At last we know, without any ifs, ands or buts, where the scheduling efforts must begin. And now what? We should examine how to exploit the constraints. Big deal. If the constraints are the client orders, exploiting the constraint means simply obeying the required delivery dates; the exploitation step is achieved by default. We can now continue into the next step of subordinating everything else to the client orders, which is not going to be as easy. We will have to spend considerable time and brain power to determine precisely how to do it.

My problem is that at the end of subordination any conflict with the data will indicate the existence of an additional constraint. We will have to identify it, but then the exploitation step is guaranteed to be anything but trivial. Following this route represents a pedagogical risk; spending a lot of time first on subordination and only then on exploitation might etch a distorted sequence in our memory. Thus, just for the sake of keeping me happy, why don't we continue to look for definite constraints before going to the next step of exploiting what we already found. This will cause us to spend a lot of effort first on the exploitation step and only then on subordination.

Can we, even theoretically, find any additional constraint at this early stage? Yes, sometimes we might find ourselves in a situation where a bottleneck does exist. Remember, we could simply continue and we would, no doubt, find out about it at the end of the first round, when subordination would have indicated violations with the data. But let's try to deal with it right now. It will make no difference to the end result, but it will help to clarify the process.

How can we identify even bottlenecks at this early stage? For that we will have to supply the system with another parameter. You see, a bottleneck is a resource that does not have enough productive capacity. In what time frame? If a time frame is not specified, then an unlimited time frame with finite market demand implies that every resource has sufficient capacity. Thus, whenever market demand is specified by a set of given orders, only when the time frame is also specified is there any point in talking about a bottleneck.

Should we choose the time frame as the time interval from present until the most remote due-date of the specified orders? That will almost guarantee that in real-life situations our attempts to find a bottleneck will end with empty hands. Let's not forget that usually our knowledge about the future is degrading as we look further and further down the road; the amount of orders that we have in hand does not encompass all the orders that we will receive in the future. Usually when we examine the orders on hand, we tend to see a heavy concentration of orders for the near future, a concentration that becomes more and more diluted as we shift our attention to more remote time horizons. Of course, what is called near future and more remote time horizons is strongly dependent on the type of industry that we are dealing with: in defense-type industries, one year is considered to be the very close future, while in a small job shop even one month might be considered as too remote. Thus, if we insist on finding a resource constraint before we attempt to exploit and subordinate to the market constraints, the only practical way left is to ask the user to specify a cut-off date, a date that we'll refer to as "schedule horizon."

To check whether or not we have a bottleneck, we first have to calculate the total load placed on each one of the the resource types, load generated by the orders that should be worked on during the "schedule horizon." What are those orders? Definitely the ones whose due-date is before the date of the schedule horizon—but that is not enough. Consider, for example, an order that must be delivered one day after the date of the schedule horizon; do we really mean that all the work needed to satisfy that order must be done only on the last day? You see, even an order that has to be delivered after the schedule horizon can place a load within the horizon. How far into the future should we go? What are the criteria? Unfortunately, it looks as though the new parameter—"schedule horizon"—didn't help us after all.

Why do we need all this headache? At the end, we know that if we do have resource constraints, we are bound to identify them sooner or later through our iterative process. Why don't we stick to the already identified market constraint and continue from there? Moreover, we're already starting to get the very erroneous impression that only firm orders should be taken into account. Let's not forget that most managerial "what if" questions must have a much longer horizon, and thus our analysis should be based on "sales forecast" as well. Thus, whenever we talk about orders, we always mean firm orders plus forecast.

Looking back on the last page, wouldn't we be much better off discarding this entire futile and pedagogical exercise? It seems to lead us only into blind alleys. Wait, not so fast! One tiny stumbling block should not cause such an outburst. Maybe one more minute of thinking will be enough to clearly show us the way.

So, which orders with due-dates after the schedule horizon should we consider in calculating the load? Orders of which we are sure that the work to fulfill them should be done within the horizon. Fine, but how do we identify them? As a matter of fact it's not too difficult; we just have to remind ourselves of what we said a few chapters ago. Any constraint should be buffered; we buffer with time. A market constraint should be buffered by a "shipping buffer." Do you recall all of these details? We said that the "material" should be released to operations an interval of time (called shipping buffer) before the due-date of the order. We also said that the actual time to do the work is negligible compared to the elapsed time, which is consumed mainly by Murphy. Thus any order whose due-date is earlier than the schedule horizon plus the shipping buffer should place its load on the company's resources within the horizon.

Now it is clear that we should consider all orders whose due dates are earlier than the schedule horizon plus shipping buffer. It is also clear that we should net out all the work that has already been done on those orders. This implies that the mechanism to calculate the relevant load must be done through exploding down from the orders to the relevant product's structures, taking into account all existing stocks, finished goods as well as work in process.

What about set-up times? Shouldn't we take them into account? Yes, but we have to be careful at this initial stage to take each set-up only once. Let's clarify this issue in somewhat more detail. Since we explode from each order, it is possible that we are going to encounter the exact same operation, on the exact same part, more than once. Different orders might have different dates, but this fact does not yet imply that we are going to produce the items for each order separately. For reasons of saving set-up time, we might elect to combine many batches into one single batch; satisfying many orders, having many different due dates, by activating the resource on the relevant part-number/operation only once. The number of set-ups that we are going to incur—and thus the size of the batches—is a function of constructing the schedule itself and thus cannot be predetermined.

The maximum that we can do at this early stage is to consider only one set-up per part-number/operation, unrelated to the number of orders requiring this particular task (assuming that at least one order requires this task). As a matter of fact, even this precaution doesn't make me too happy. We all know that process times are not exactly accurate, but set-up time estimations resemble, in most cases, just wild guesses. What can we do about it? As we are going to see very soon, we will have to choose at this stage, anyhow, one bottleneck, maximum. If we can find a bottleneck without relying on any set up-data, that's preferable. This means that we'll regard set-up as part of the constraint identification only as a last resort.

Once the load is calculated for each type of resource, we'll have to calculate their availability during the same (present to schedule horizon without shipping buffer) future time interval, according to the given calendars. Of course, the number of units that the company has for each type of resource must be taken into account when availability is calculated. If the load placed on any resource is greater than its availability, we do have at least one bottleneck.

30. *How to work with very inaccurate data*

Suppose that when we compare the two lists, the one displaying the load per type of resource to the list displaying the resource availability, we find that every resource type has more than enough capacity. So what? We cannot conclude anything about the existence of resource constraints, but no harm has been done. Remember that since all required data resides in memory, all this explosion work (which is basically equivalent to performing full net requirement) didn't take any significant time. However, what should we do if not one but several resources turn out to have less available time than is needed to fulfill the orders?

In such a case, we certainly have a resource constraint, but how many? Should we declare each one of those problematic resources as a constraint? Definitely not! Out of this list we might find that we have one, and only one, resource constraint. Remember how dangerous it is to declare as a constraint something that is actually not! So let's be very careful. First let's clarify how it can be that even though the calculation clearly indicates that a resource does not have enough capacity to fulfill all market demands, nevertheless it might be a non-constraint.

Suppose that we are dealing with the trivial case where we have to deliver only one product. The orders are for 100 units to be delivered each day for the next ten days. The production process of this product is very simple: each unit involves ten different operations to be done in series (one after the other), and each operation requires a different type of resource. In our company there is only one unit per each type of resource, and each resource is available for 24 hours a day. Let's suppose that each operation requires at least one hour to perform, and the longest takes two hours. Now let's calculate the load placed on each resource due to the orders, and compare it to the resource's availability. In our case the comparison clearly indicates that each and every resource type does not have sufficient capacity.

Does this mean that all of them are constraints, that all resources are limiting the ability of our company to make more money? Not at all. If we cannot possibly get additional capacity, the resource that will dictate the end result will be the resource that requires two hours per unit. All other resources will not have any impact on the end result. If we cannot get more capacity for this specific resource, we can even double the capacity of all the others and it won't change the end result. Thus, we can see that if we have more than one resource that does not have sufficient capacity to satisfy all market demands, nevertheless, there might be only one resource constraint.

Therefore, from all the resources that do not have sufficient capacity, only the resource that lacks capacity the most can at this stage be declared as a suspected resource constraint. Suspected, we said. Why can't we declare it as a definite constraint? Because this analysis is based on the available data, and we know that this type of data might be grossly inaccurate.

What is the situation that we are facing right now? We identified the orders as a constraint, and we have reason to believe that on top of that we have a resource constraint. If it turns out that we are right, that we do have a resource constraint and we are unable to satisfy the market constraint due to lack of capacity, this means that we are facing a situation where we have a conflict between the company's constraints. Any resolution of this conflict will yield a degradation in the company's performance. Shouldn't we, before compromising on the company's performance, at least check whether or not the situation is based on erroneous data?

But let's face it, after more than two decades of trying, almost desperately, to keep accurate records, we have learned that it is virtually impossible to keep all process times accurately. So, what are we supposed to do?

Let's remind ourselves that even though it is not feasible to ensure the accuracy of all process times, nevertheless it is quite easy to verify the validity of just a few.

What data elements have brought us to suspect the existence of a particular resource constraint? Let's examine them, bearing in mind that different types of data might have different probabilities of being inaccurate. Our calculation was based on the computation of resource-type availability and on their required load. The availability computation was based, in turn, on the calendar and on the data of the number of units available from this resource type. The calendar is usually uniform for the entire organization, or at least to large sections of it, and thus it is usually very thoroughly checked. The chance that we will find a mistake here is quite small.

But that is not the case when we regard the accuracy of the number of resource units. As strange as it might sound, this piece of data is usually subject to gross mistakes. Not too surprising when we recall that the numbers of resource units are of no use in calculating net requirement or in cost calculations, so today, nobody is bothering to update these numbers. Moreover, it is quite common to find, at the top of our list, resources that simply do not exist. They are just phantoms, introduced in order to enable the system personnel to circumvent their own rigid system.

Of course, whenever we find such a gross mistake, we'll correct it and re-examine our list. Suppose that now the data regarding the availability of the suspected resource constraint has been checked and found to be accurate. What should we check now? The data that we used to calculate the load. Which elements of the data do we feel most uneasy with? Of course, the process times. All of them? Certainly not, only the process times that are required from that particular resource. Can we narrow it down even further? Yes, the process time of the tasks performed by this particular resource, for which there is at least one demand within the time frame that the user chooses to consider. Are all of them important to the same degree? No, some tasks will require a big chunk of time while others will absorb only a few hours. On what does it depend? On the time to process a single unit and the quantities required by the orders.

This line of reasoning looks very obvious, almost infantile. Why do we bother to elaborate at such length? Because, unfortunately, the current situation is that whenever we suspect that our data is not in good shape, and is leading us to erroneous conclusions, the common practice is just to declare "the data must be cleaned"—usually with the additional warning of "to a level of at least 95%," leaving the user with that mess. Any system that treats the data accuracy problem in this way simply ignores one of its most important functions—to highlight, in a very clear and precise way, which data elements, out of the entire maze, should be checked, narrowing it down to the extent that the job of verifying data accuracy will become feasible. What we are doing right now is demonstrating that a system can do it, provided that the designers of the system will give this subject the appropriate importance.

So, where do we stand now? It is quite clear that the system should display to the user a chart detailing which tasks are absorbing what percent of the availability of our suspected constraint. We are dealing here with loosely connected variables, and thus it is reasonable to expect that just a few tasks are creating the majority of the load. Those tasks' process times, and those alone, should be verified by the user. Usually we will need to check about five or so process times.

Remember, it's always preferable to do the check with the people who are performing the tasks and not with the people who designed them. The rule among experienced MRP consultants is, "Always check with the foreman, not with the engineer. The foreman, most probably, will cheat you—about thirty percent. But you know exactly in which direction he is cheating. The engineer might mislead you, even by as much as two hundred percent, and you don't have even the foggiest idea in which direction."

Once the relevant process times are checked (assuming that no gross mistake has been found), now is the time to verify, for those "big-load tasks" only, the corresponding client orders. It is not uncommon to find, in the order's quantity, a mistake of some order of magnitude—a stray zero has been key-punched by a bored clerk.

What is the recommended way for the information system to distill those data elements? The first tendency is to store all this data as the system carries out the explosions needed to calculate the loads. Certainly at that stage, all the data is "visited" and can be easily recorded. But this is the wrong thing to do. Just ask yourself, "If we do capture the data at the explosion stage, how much data has to be stored, and what little portion of it will eventually need to be displayed?"

Here is a very good example of how to cause the entire system to respond at a snail's pace. Remember the vast difference between the computer speed in storing/retrieving versus its speed in calculating. If we store per each resource all the relevant tasks together with their process times, and on top of it we store, for each of those tasks, all the code names of the corresponding client orders, then there is no doubt that even for a relatively small company, there will not be enough on-line memory. Sixteen megabytes of on-line memory (the current maximum available on PC's) will be far from sufficient. If we try to store all of it on disks, the elapsed time will be much too long.

The answer lies in the direction that we already outlined. Since all the relevant basic data already resides in memory, there is no point in storing intermediate results. Simply recalculate them. For the suspected resource constraint, let's implode from all its tasks (part-number/operation that requires this particular resource) toward the orders level. This step will establish the product connections between our resource constraint and the corresponding market constraints. For the sake of simplicity, let's refer to these product connections as to "red lanes," as if we painted those sections of the product structure with imaginary red paint.

Now, we can explode down from the corresponding orders along just the red lanes, and store the loads (and not the orders data) that we need for the load chart mentioned above. This is a relatively small amount of data and will not represent any significant demand on the available on-line memory. Only when the user wants to see the details of the corresponding client orders and for the specific task that the user is interested in, only for that task will we implode to find and display the content of the orders. It looks like too many redundant explosions and implosions, but remember each such activity takes seconds, or even less. It definitely will require more programming effort, but what is more important—the programmer's one-time effort or the constant drain on the user's time and patience?

So, once we pass the stage of verifying the very few data elements that caused us to suspect the existence of a resource constraint, only then are we in the unenviable position where we have to sort out an apparent conflict between the company's constraints. How is an information system supposed to handle it? Just throw it back into the user's lap? What is he/she going to do then? No, here comes a real test of our information system, narrowing down the conflict to its basic bare roots, so that we, the users, will face very clear alternatives. So clear that we will not have any real difficulty choosing between them, using just our intuition.

31. *Pinpointing the conflicts between the identified constraints*

Identifying a bottleneck means that we cannot satisfy all orders on their respective demanded dates; we simply do not have enough available capacity, at least on one resource—something will have to give. It is also apparent that the information system doesn't have the required data to make the appropriate decision, even if—by some miracle—we succeed in building into it the required smarts.

Which client will be less upset if we do not deliver on time? Can we ease the pressure by partial shipment? If so, to whom and how much? And what about some alternative modes of execution? Usually undesirable modes, but not when the alternative is to lose a client. Yes, it's impossible to ask the people to work once again on the weekend, we're not even going to consider it, except for . . . and so on. No, it is totally unrealistic to expect all this voluminous and vague data to be fed to the system.

What we need is a way in which the information system will be able to focus the conflict, so that those types of decisions can be done easily, not by the system itself, but by the responsible managers.

How are we going to go about it? Why don't we use our tried and true path, namely: the five focusing steps.

But haven't we already identified the constraints? Don't we already have a conflict between the identified constraints? Never mind. The fact is we are confused, which is exactly the most appropriate time to follow the focusing steps.

Let's start with the first constraint we identified, the market constraint; and now let's move to the second step, EXPLOIT. This simply means that we would like to meet all the required due-dates on time. Fine. Now, let's SUBORDINATE. We are supposed to check, at the end of this step, whether or not we have generated a conflict. We are already aware of such a conflict, a conflict with the limited availability of a particular resource. So, rather than trying to subordinate the entire company to the exploitation decision, let's concentrate only on subordinating the action of the specific resource. Let's find out the exact details of the resulting conflict.

What is the meaning of subordinating a resource? It means ignoring any of its own limitations and concentrating on finding out exactly what we would like that resource to do in order to satisfy the constraint. Nice. So, given a specific order, what would we like our resource to do in order to satisfy it? To perform its needed work; to produce the appropriate number of units required to fulfill the order. Fine. How many units? Well, it depends.

Oh, come on. I'm your obedient resource. I'm willing to do whatever you tell me, so please tell me. Not by throwing clues and hints—just tell me in a straightforward manner, using specific numbers whenever possible.

OK, we got the message. We are talking, all of a sudden, to a computer—to a totally obedient moron, which is probably what we should pretend when we are trying to devise a very rigorous procedure. How many units does the resource have to produce? That is quite easy to figure out. Start with the order's required quantity, and exploding through the product structure, translate this number into the units required from the resource. Let's not forget that in the product structure the "quantity per," written on the connecting arrows, might differ from one. For example, if the order is for cars and our resource has to produce the wheels, than an order for 100 cars is translated into a requirement to produce 400 wheels. Or, if the order is for twenty bolts, it might be translated into the need to prepare one invoice document.

That by itself is not enough. We might have, on the product structure, some data regarding expected scrap. Thus we might find that in order to deliver to the client 100 units, the resource will have to be instructed to produce not 100 but 110 units. Now, are we happy with the answer?

Not quite. You see, we cannot assume that we start with a clean slate, with empty pipelines. What about the tasks that, at the time of constructing the schedule, are already stuck somewhere between our resource and the orders? We will need to net these stocks out, which is exactly what we did when the expected load on the resources was calculated.

Yes, but now we face a new problem. How are we going to allocate those stocks? When we considered the total load it didn't matter, but here we are dealing with determining the detailed instructions. To what order should we allocate a particular amount of stock, if it is enough to cover some of the relevant orders but not all of them?

This is an excellent example of how to take a small pussycat and try to present it as a fierce tiger, making a big deal out of some trivial, well-established technical procedures. What are we trying to do? To impress everybody by how technically competent we are? I thought that we agreed that our discussion would be aimed at revealing how an information system can be built; have we already forgotten this original target?

The above is also an example of how easy is it to be drowned in details, drowned to the extent that not only the total picture becomes obliterated, but it also opens the gates to super "sophistication"—sophistication that might ruin the usability of the package. How to allocate the stocks? According to the required dates of the orders. The one with the early due-date wins over the order with the later date. There is no point in using more sophisticated rules. Don't try to decide which order is more important. Anyhow, this type of data will never be reliably available to a mechanized system. Don't try to consider lead-time from the stock to the order; anyhow, those lead times are mainly a function of dear old Murphy. Don't try to be overly smart; the end result will always prove you wrong. We, at least, are going to stick to basics. "First come, first served" is a fine and simple rule.

What an outrage! Will you please calm down. I just wanted to honestly find out how to subordinate the resource constraint to the decision to exploit the market constraint. Maybe for you it is trivial, but don't ignore the fact that I'm doing such things for the first time. It's hard enough to visualize what is actually meant by "explosions" and "implosions." You don't have to make things even more difficult by showing your impatience.

Shall we carry on?

Slowly, please.

We have calculated the quantity our resource has to do in order to satisfy a particular order. From that, using the time required to perform one unit and the set-up time, we can easily conclude the amount of load that will be required from the resource. Now, what is left to do is to find out where to place this load on the time axis—to determine WHEN the resource has to perform, so that the given order will be satisfied, considering no limitations due to the resource itself.

This question is quite easy to answer. We have the required due-date of the order, we also have been given, by the user, the length of the shipping buffer—the amount of time that we have to allow for the task to reach its destination safely. Thus we should "release" the task from the resource constraint a shipping buffer before it's due to be shipped. In other words, ideally, the resource constraint should complete its job a shipping buffer before the order's due-date.

What we have to do now is to repeat the same calculation for all orders demanding work from our resource constraint, placing their resulting "blocks" of work on the resource's time axis. For each order we have to perform the allocation of the intermediate stocks, and to generate the blocks—why don't we combine the two efforts to be done in one step. Since we chose to allocate according to the orders' due-dates, the easiest way to perform all this work is to start with the earliest order, and moving forward in time, deal with each order in its turn. For each order for which there is not enough stock in the pipe we'll have to generate the block of work needed from the resource constraint.

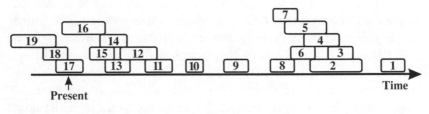

11   The "ruins."

Of course, since we place the blocks of work without considering the resource's own limitations, these blocks might pile up on top of each other. We are probably going to get a picture like the one presented in Figure 11, a picture that resembles "ruins." A totally unrealistic scenario. It is unrealistic to expect a resource to perform more than one block at a time, so if we have, for example, only one unit of that resource type, a pile of blocks of work is out of the question.

We are facing a conflict. Not a big surprise, we were expecting a conflict, and now is the time to try and resolve it. We must "level the ruins." We must make sure that the amount of blocks that are required to be done at the same point in time will never exceed the number of units available on the resource constraint. This means that whenever we encounter an accumulation, we have to shift the upper blocks. Which side of the ruin should we shift them to? Should we postpone their execution? That obviously won't do; by shifting a block forward in time, we endanger the shipping date of the corresponding order. So, let's level the ruins by shifting the upper blocks to the left, making them earlier than strictly demanded by the orders' due-dates. It really means increasing inventory, but this is better than losing throughput.

So, let's imagine a big bulldozer standing at the right of our ruins picture. Let's adjust its huge blade to be at a height equal to the number of the available resource units. Now, instruct the bulldozer to move to the left, leveling the ground. Our bulldozer is a very unique instrument. It keeps the order (the sequence) of the blocks; a block whose right edge is appearing after (later) the right edge of another block, will keep its relative position, even after the bulldozer has leveled the ground. To turn this figurative picture into a computer code is very easy, so it's not necessary to elaborate on those very technical details. One outburst was more than enough.

But wait, we haven't finished. We haven't removed the conflict, we just pushed it to another place. Since we are dealing with a resource that does not have enough capacity, it's unavoidable that the end result of the work of our magnificent bulldozer is that we'll find some blocks on the wrong side of the time axis. Blocks of work will, unavoidably, be pushed to the past. We cannot command a resource to do work yesterday, that's obvious. Moreover, our bulldozer technique will make things even worse. Depending on the pattern of the orders it might leave some gaps at the right, and make things worse where it really counts, at the left of our picture.

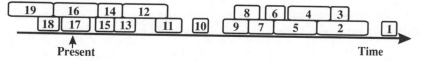
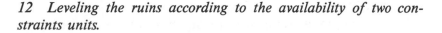

12 Leveling the ruins according to the availability of two constraints units.

Worse? Not quite, just a more precise presentation of the conflict. At this stage it seems unavoidable that we must yield to reality—we definitely cannot do things in the past. Some orders' due-dates will have to start to give. Let's take our bulldozer. Right now it is parked at the left of our picture; turn it around and lower the blade so it will represent an iron wall. Now, let's command it to move, to push the blocks to the right, to push up to the point that no order will have to be worked on in the past. By the last move we have avoided the possibility of clashing with reality, but what happens to the orders' due-dates?

Of course these bulldozer manipulations, moving orders first to the past, then to the future, will leave the blocks in different locations than their original starting point. Since we have started with a constraint resource, it is mandatory that some blocks will end up later (to the right) than their original position. This means that their corresponding orders are now exposed. If the resulting shift is by more than half the buffer, the company's chance of missing the due-date of the corresponding order is not just quite high; count on Murphy to turn it into certainty. Thus, rather than filling the entire computer screen with data, let's just color the endangering blocks red. A system doing all the above will provide the user with a very precise and concentrated picture of the conflict between the company's constraints.

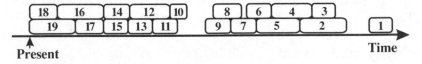
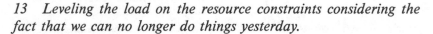

Present   Time

13 Leveling the load on the resource constraints considering the fact that we can no longer do things yesterday.

Should we leave it like this, waiting for the user to intervene? Not yet. We still have something to do; but before we continue, why don't we take some time to digest the above interesting mechanism. It's not identical to any scheduling technique we have ever seen. It cannot even be placed under the previous two main groups of scheduling methods—the backward- or forward-in-time methods. As a matter of fact, from what has been described so far, it is obvious that this method does not even use the time axis as the main driving force in scheduling. This technique, so far, is simply a direct, almost blunt, derivation of the five focusing steps, which in turn, let's not forget, are a direct, logical deduction from the choice of THROUGHPUT as the number-one measurement.

Let's spend some time viewing the relevant graphs: Figure 11 displays the original "ruins"; Figure 12 displays the results of the first pass of the "bulldozer"; and Figure 13 presents the current end result. Can you picture what would be the result if, instead of a bottleneck, we dealt with a resource that on the average has sufficient capacity, but not at specific intervals of time? It looks like we now have the generic method to deal with any type of resource constraint. Of course, we still have to explore the general procedure of how to subordinate not just the resource constraints but all resources, but we are getting there. We definitely are.

32. *Starting to remove conflicts—the system/user interplay*

Where have we left the user? Oh yes, staring at a screen which displays the resource constraint's blocks of work, some painted with warning red, which indicates that their corresponding orders are going to be late. We cannot leave the situation as is, and the easy way out, instructing the resource to start earlier, simply cannot be used in this case. No red block, if of course we haven't made any logical or computational mistake, can be moved to the left. The way in which we sequenced the tasks guarantees that our resource is totally busy, doing other, even more urgent blocks, from the present until any red block. It seems that the only way to deliver this particular order on time is to violate something else; either give it priority over another earlier order, which means that that order will be late, or to increase the available capacity of the resource, or to . . .

As we said before, all those types of manipulations can be done, not by our information system, but by the user himself. But wait, before we hand the ball over to the user, have we finished everything that we should do? Not quite. We might have, on one hand, presented the user with just a partial picture —the actual situation might be even worse than presented. On the other hand, we might still be able to help resolve the conflicts.

First, let's check if the picture presented really took everything that we knew into account. What bothers us is the fact that in order to exploit the resource constraint, we instructed it to work from the present. Have we checked that such instructions can be fulfilled, that the appropriate materials needed to carry out these tasks are actually there, waiting for the constraint? Because if this is not the case, what are the chances that within minutes they will become available? Are we launching instructions to the constraint to carry out work that is, at this stage, an impossibility? To launch a schedule where, already in the first step, a constraint has to improvise, is not launching a schedule, it more resembles launching chaos.

Can we take such a consideration into account? Of course. All the needed data is at our disposal. We do know what material, and how much of it, is waiting now right in front of the constraint. So what we have to do is to perform some further small manipulations on the picture appearing on the screen. We have to make sure that the first blocks do have their corresponding material already waiting. This means that if, right now, this is not the case, the system has to look for the earliest required blocks for which the material is available and re-sequence them to be at the very start.

What should we call the start? What period of starting time should we protect by scheduling there blocks that already have available material? Enough to enable bringing whatever else is needed. Very nice answer, but do we have even a clue of this time interval? Yes, more than just a clue. We were given, by the user, the estimation of the resource-constraint buffer. This is the estimation of the time needed for a task to be brought from release to the resource constraint, to be brought with very high probability and without any hassle. Should we transfer this know-how, as is, to our situation? Let's not forget that here we are under pressure, we are postponing urgent things. OK, let's then say that since it is urgent and we are willing to expedite, we should protect blocks only to the extent that they have to be done no later than half the resource-constraint buffer from the present. Why half, why not two-thirds of the buffer? Starting by improvising on the constraint is certainly going to cause more than just one order to be shipped late. Fine, let it be two-thirds. But after this period of time, we can safely assume that whatever materials are needed, we'll have already succeeded in bringing to the constraint. Thus, we can schedule the resource constraint from there on, without being concerned with the present availability of materials.

We are now quite protected, but won't all this additional shuffling just enhance our problems? Won't it create even more red blocks? Probably so, but this is reality. It is unrealistic to plan work when material is unavailable, just to present a better picture. The user will have to resolve all the red blocks, including the one that we just now created. Can we lend a helping hand? Yes, certainly; but remember, at this stage more than ever, our information system must take the back seat; the user must be firmly in the driver's seat.

When set-up time is required from our resource constraint, there is a remote possibility to enhance throughput without clashing into the boundaries of necessary conditions. Enhance throughput by saving some restricted amount of set-up, so that the only penalty will be paying just with increased inventory. We said that whenever the trade-off is between throughput and inventory, our system should do it without asking further permission. We said it, and nevertheless here we are going to deviate from this rule.

Here, anyway, the user will have to manipulate the sequence manually. This throughput enhancement opportunity that we are going to discuss now will, in most cases, not be sufficient to resolve all conflicts, and thus we'll need to stop the run and bother the user. Moreover, at the same time, we can achieve the improvement only by changing the natural sequence of the blocks. They will no longer follow the orders' due-dates, and thus it will be more confusing to the user to get a firm handle on the additional required changes. Thus, I believe that it is better to present the user with the "raw" picture and to ask for a direct instruction to perform the trivial set-up savings.

What is this opportunity that we mentioned, what do we call

trivial set-up savings? Whenever there are two identical blocks, there is the possibility to save set-up. Identical blocks means that two different orders need execution of the same part-number/operation. Each block contains a provision for set-up, unless the two blocks are done consecutively, one immediately following the other. In such cases there is no need to reset the resource, and thus there is no provision for set-up on the second block. Therefore moving one of two identical blocks so that they will be produced consecutively will enable "gluing" of the blocks, which frees up capacity, enabling the constraint to satisfy more orders within the same time interval.

What are the negatives? One is that in order to "glue" blocks, we'll have to jump the later block backward in time, to make it earlier than otherwise needed (to move the early block forward, would mean to delay the shipment of its corresponding order). This means that we'll release inventory sooner to the operations. Inventory, due to the desire to save set-up, will be increased. If this will help to ship other orders on time, we are glad to pay the price of increased inventory. Of course, this means that if we try to "glue" two identical blocks where the situation is that after the later block there are no red blocks, it's a clear indication that we lost sight of the goal. Whom is this set-up "savings" going to help? Are we going to ship more, to increase throughput?

If inventory increase were the only negative, we would do the gluing as a common practice. We are all aware of many cases where the set-up time is quite large and there are many orders for "onesies" and "twosies" that require ridiculously short process times. In those cases if we don't glue blocks, we face a situation where the vast majority of the resource constraint's time is devoted not for production but for set-up. Why then do we refer to this set-up time savings as a small enhancement? The answer lies in the fact that we are not against gluing blocks, we are against allowing the information system to do it without a careful monitoring by the user. In most cases set-up savings carries a penalty which is bigger than just increasing inventory. Let's investigate it in more depth.

When we glue two blocks, all blocks that are supposed to be done after the second block will gain; they are going to be worked on earlier than if the gluing hadn't taken place. They will be done earlier by an amount of time equal to the saved set-up time. But what about all the blocks that were between the two glued blocks? All those blocks will be done later. Their execution will be postponed by the amount of time needed to produce the second block, the one that jumped the queue. If we are dealing with a case where between the two identical blocks there is even one red block, gluing the identical blocks means that we assume the knowledge of which order is more important to fulfill on time. This type of decision should not be done by the information system.

Nevertheless, there are enough situations where the user will have to make such decisions. Is the system going to allow such gluing to be done only manually? In some not too rare situations, manual manipulations—dealing with each block separately—will drive the user nuts. We must provide mechanized help. Moreover, remember that each time we save a set-up, we don't change the situation of just one block, we affect many blocks. And as we said, some will turn red and others will hopefully become pale. It is evident that we must provide some means by which the user can give, not block by block instructions, but a much broader instruction, and be able to see the impact of his/her instruction on all the points of conflict.

What type of a general instruction might be appropriate? The gluing of blocks is more important when the set-up times are relatively big. Let's not forget that the set-up is not just a function of the resource but also a function of the specific task the resource is supposed to carry out. Thus, even though we are dealing here with one resource type, different blocks will represent bigger or smaller opportunities for set-up savings. On the other hand, in order to save set-up, we have to reach into the future and bring from there a block. The further we reach, the more blocks there will be that are going to suffer due to this maneuver (all the blocks that are between the original block and the one that we jump backward).

Thus, it is reasonable to ask the user to give a general instruction expressed as a number which represents a ratio, the ratio between the time that is going to be saved and the time that the system is allowed to reach into the future. For example, a number 100 will be interpreted as the instruction: for each one hour of set-up saved, the system is allowed to bring a block that is remote from its identical block a maximum of 100 hours in the future.

Since most users have never had the opportunity to see the impact of such a trade-off on their own operation, this number should not be given as an input parameter, but rather the user must have the ability to try, on-line, several numbers until he/ she is satisfied by the projected picture of the blocks' colors. Since the execution of one such instruction (attempting to see the impact of one suggested number on the colors of all blocks) should not take more than several seconds, we are dealing here with a real decision-support system—one that is designed not to ignore the fact that human intuition cannot always be expressed in numbers, and at the same time, does not "help" by presenting known data but by presenting the results of the user's alternative decision.

Have we, in this stage, removed all the conflicts? Have we eliminated red from the screen? Certainly not. We have probably reduced the number of red blocks, but we still have a few; remember, we know that we are dealing with a bottleneck. As a matter of fact, in those situations where we don't have any significant set-up on the resource constraint, we haven't yet done a thing to remove the conflicts.

So, now is the time to use a bigger gun. Overtime.

33. *Resolving all remaining conflicts*

As we mentioned before, the system should provide, as part of the inputs, the ability to give some broad guidelines of overtime allowed per resource. These guidelines are given with the understanding that overtime will be used only in cases where otherwise throughput would be jeopardized, and not for any other artificial purpose.

The overtime instructions are given in the form of limitations: how many hours maximum are allowed per day, per weekend, and how many hours maximum are allowed per week. The need for the requirement to specify a number for the week is due to the fact that sometimes the hours allowed per week are smaller than just the multiplication of the day's allotment by the number of working days plus the number specified for the weekend. People fatigue is a major consideration.

As we are going to see later, the overtime instructions, as far as the non-constraint resources are concerned, are going to be obeyed without the need for additional permission from the user. This is not the case when we are dealing with a resource that has been identified as a constraint; here we were engaged in trying to save set-up time. Only after those attempts have been exhausted by the user is there any point in trying to inject overtime, and thus an initiative by the user is required.

What we have to bear in mind is that whenever we allow overtime on a specific date, what is going to be helped by the overtime is not only the blocks that are supposed to be completed at the end of this date; all other blocks that are supposed to be done later are going to benefit—all could be done earlier than already planned. Thus, we might face the situation where, when we give some overtime to help a specific red block, this block might remain red, but many other blocks, later blocks, might change from red to normal. Moreover, this last observation indicates that in order to "help" a specific block we can use overtime not only on the date it is supposed to be completed, but on all other earlier dates. Of course the earlier that we give the overtime relative to the date of the block, the more we increase the inventory in the company.

Now it seems that we are ready to instruct even a dumb computer how to assign overtime. What is needed is to translate what we have just said into logically derived actions. We said that overtime permissions are to be used only for enhancing throughput; thus, the trigger to consider overtime should be red blocks on our screen. If none of the blocks are red, no order is in danger of being late—why should we even consider overtime?

Which red block should we consider first? We said that an hour of overtime given at a specific date helps, to exactly the same degree, not just one block but all blocks which are supposed to be completed at a later date. We don't want to waste overtime (remember that unlike regular hours, every hour of overtime is increasing operating expense) and thus we'd better place it where it helps the most, namely before the first red block. We also said that the earlier the date at which the overtime is given, from the date of the red block, the bigger the penalty we pay in increased inventory. Thus we should not just place the overtime before (to the left of) the first red block, we have to place it as close as possible to that block.

So let's start by concentrating on just the first red block, ignoring the other blocks. Let's move backward in time from that block, giving overtime wherever permitted. We'll continue to do so until one of two things happens: either the red block will change its color or, unfortunately, we'll hit the present. Of course, if the latter condition has stopped us, it means that we have exhausted the overtime avenue as a way to help the corresponding order, and we'll have to ask the user for more drastic means.

Have we finished? Not yet; remember our screen looks as if it has the measles. The red block that we have dealt with was not the only one, it was just the first of many. True, the overtime that we already allowed has certainly helped all the other nasty red blocks, some even turned pale. But, nevertheless, usually it was not enough, and many red blocks are still coloring our screen. What the system has to do is simply to repeat the same process, this time concentrating on the next closest red block, which by definition must reside, if at all, to the right of our original (hopefully no longer red) block. The system should continue dancing this interesting dance, one step forward—to the next still red block—many steps backward—to plug in the overtime wherever permitted—until it deals with all the red blocks.

If the situation is really bad, or if overtime possibilities are very slim, we'll end up still having red spots disturbing the otherwise nice screen. Now we have to turn to "individual" treatment. The user can still manipulate the screen. He/she can decide to off-load a particular block to be done by another resource, split a block and remove part of it to be done at a different time, or decide on a much bigger, one-time shot of overtime. Everything goes; the user is the real boss.

This "individual" treatment should be correctly understood. The actions are aimed at solving a problem of a particular red block, but that doesn't mean that they have an impact on just that block. The opposite is usually correct. For example, off-loading a particular block to another (non-constraint) work center will definitely help this particular order, but it will also improve the situation of all red blocks whose execution date is later than the off-loaded block. This means that in order to see the impact of the user decision, the screen presenting the updated situation of all the constraint's blocks is very important, actually vital. This time dependent block presentation turns out to be more effective than originally envisioned.

Being so happy with all these possibilities should not blind us from recognizing the most important alternative open to the user; the user can always give up. No, this is not a joke. Even though there are still red blocks on the screen, the user can choose to say, "I've done everything humanly possible; I will have to live with some late orders." Such a statement means that there aren't any recognized ways to remove the conflicts through dealing with the limited capacity of the resource constraint. Thus the only way left to remove the conflicts is by postponing the promised due-date of the corresponding orders.

The system must now do exactly that. The due-date of each order which created a red block must now be pushed into the future. By how much? The new due-date must be set to be equal to the ending time of the latest among its red blocks, plus the shipping buffer. The orders that have been affected should be displayed. Many times, when we realize the magnitude of the delays, we all of a sudden find more "innovative" ways to provide more capacity. The user must be presented with the end results, then given the opportunity to go back and continue to struggle with the red blocks.

We don't like to miss due-dates, but there is something that we should dread even more—to miss a due-date without giving the client any warning. What is the situation here? We don't have enough capacity, we have already tried everything that we could think of, and we are still short. Unless a miracle happens, we are definitely going to miss some due-dates. It's much better to call now, a few weeks in advance, and deliver the bad news to the client. It is better by far than apologizing after the fact.

Once this step is completed, we have actually completed our first attempt at what is usually referred to as the "master schedule." Notice, this master schedule differs from the generally accepted concept in one important point. It is created not only from data regarding orders, but also from data regarding the detailed schedule of the resource constraint.

Why are we so careful to refer to it as only a "first attempt"?

Because we haven't finished yet. There might be more resource constraints. So now we have to perform the next step: SUBOR-DINATE EVERYTHING ELSE TO THE ABOVE DECISION. The actions of all other resources will need to be derived, so that they will safely support what we have already decided.

In a way, what we have done is to fix some activities firmly on to the time axis, and we made sure that no internal conflicts exist. Now, all other activities have to march in accordance. This is why we refer to the stage we just finished as "authorizing the DRUM." We have determined the drum beat to which the entire company will have to march.

Before we dive in and begin to figure out the appropriate procedure to subordinate all other resources, maybe it would behoove us to introduce, at this point, a new concept—the concept of RODS. Actually, in most environments it does not have any applicability at this stage, but there are some where it does, and a few where it is dominant. Moreover, in all environments the ROD concept is vital when a second resource constraint is identified, so why don't we deal with it right now.

We might face situations where a resource constraint is called on to perform work on more than just one stage of the same task. In such a case, the same order will generate more than one block on our drum. No special problem, as long as the two blocks don't feed each other through operations done by other resources. Let's review what should bother us if we do encounter a situation where a resource constraint is feeding itself through other resources. The dilemma is, of course, by how much should we protect the second (later) operation of the constraint? We can not leave it without any protection—Murphy might hit the intermediate operations—but on the other hand, to delay work already done by the constraint is also undesirable. It is apparent that we must buffer the second constraint operation, but it is also apparent that we can not afford to be very cautious, so we should not buffer it with a full constraint buffer. Protecting it with half the length of the constraint buffer looks like a reasonable compromise.

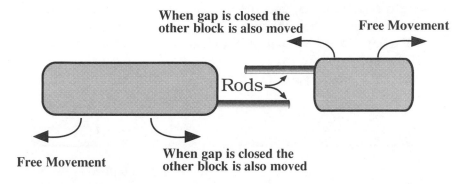

When gap is closed the other block is also moved

Free Movement

Rods

Free Movement

When gap is closed the other block is also moved

14 The rods concept.

Is that all? Not quite. In this situation we have to be careful when we move the blocks on the time axis. Moving the early block backward in time does not represent a problem, but moving it forward in time will require moving its "younger brother." The minimum time gap allowed between them is, as we said, half the resource-constraint buffer. Likewise, moving the later block backward in time will necessitate moving the "older brother." It looks as if there are "steel rods" attached to these blocks. The early block has a rod pointing forward in time, and the later block has a rod pointing backward in time. The length of each rod is equal to half the resource-constraint buffer. These blocks are allowed to move freely on the time axis, but their rods might cause their corresponding block to be moved as well. Figure 14 illustrates the situation. Of course a resource constraint might feed itself many times along the same single task, as in the electronic wafer industry, and thus a block might have more than one rod attached to it. In such a case, movement of one block might cause the movement of many.

This is all quite simple, but before we leave this subject we might peer a bit more into the length of the rod. No, I don't mean to question the somewhat arbitrary decision of half the buffer; what I refer to is the fact that we are treating the blocks as if they were a point rather than an interval in time. Let's see what we have to take into account when we recognize the length of the blocks, and the fact that two blocks might differ considerably in their length.

We have to ensure that each unit done at the early block will

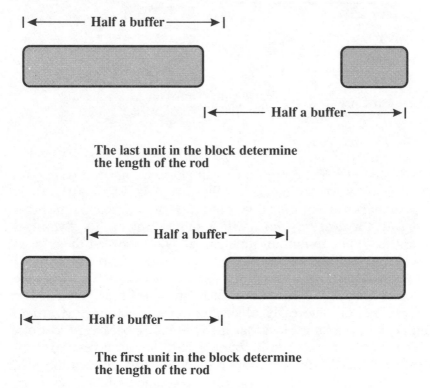

The last unit in the block determine
the length of the rod

The first unit in the block determine
the length of the rod

15

have sufficient time (half the buffer length) to arrive for its process at the later block. If the early block is much longer than the second block, and we provide just half the buffer for the first unit in the block, it will guarantee that we will be in deep trouble regarding the last unit. We also cannot choose to look only on the last unit in the block, because the situation is exactly reversed when the later block is much longer than the early one, as shown in Figure 15. The only way is to consider both ends and to calculate accordingly the minimum distance that must separate the beginning of the two blocks. This will be the effective length of the corresponding rods.

Putting this subject behind us, I feel hard pressed to find another good reason for procrastinating. It looks as if we don't have any choice but to continue to the next segment of our journey, the subject of subordination.

34. *Manual subordination: the drum-buffer-rope method*

Where are we? The due-dates for the orders and the exact dates for the resource-constraint operations (the blocks) have already been fixed in a previous step. Nor do we have to worry about any mismatch between the dates; any order's date is guaranteed to be removed from the date of its latest block by at least a shipping buffer (or in case of emergencies, by at least half a shipping buffer). Now we have to fix the dates for all other activities.

First, let's determine the dates for the release of materials, so that we are assured that they will arrive at the resource constraint on time. We have already established the rule: materials should be released to operations a resource buffer before the date they are supposed to be consumed by the resource constraint. Thus, in order to determine those material release dates, we just have to subtract the resource buffer from the dates that have already been established at the drum.

What about the dates for all intermediate operations? Let's not forget what we have agreed upon; we certainly don't want them to hold the inventory that we already decided to release. We want that inventory to accumulate before the constraints; only there does it serve as a protection against disruptions. Thus the dates of the material release are the dates that we give to the non-constraint resources that are supposed to perform the intermediate operations; we want all operations to work on the inventory as soon as it is available to them, hopefully on the date of release.

Are these resources actually going to perform their jobs on that date? We are not that naive—Murphy does exist, temporary queues are definitely going to occur. That's why we released the material so early. That means that whenever we give an instruction with a specific date to a non-constraint resource, the interpretation should not be "Do it on that day,"—not at all. The actual interpretation is "Do it as soon as you can, preferably the minute the material arrives, but if the material arrives before the specified date, please wait, don't work on it. Somebody has made a mistake. From the point of view of the entire system, bearing disruptions in mind, there is no need to work right now on these pieces. Please hold them until the specified date."

Which brings us to the conclusion that unless there is already a lot of excess inventory on the floor, there is not much point in giving schedules to the various work centers. It's enough to firmly control the release and to tell everybody else to work (in whatever sequence) on the materials that do arrive.

Everybody except, of course, the resource constraints themselves. The resource constraints should rigorously follow the sequence that we labored so hard to polish. They must try to follow it to the best of their ability, and thus they must be provided with the drum list.

Wait; there is another exception, those operations that use common parts, parts needed for more than just one part-number/operation. For the corresponding work centers, an instruction of the type "If you have material, work on it," might lead to divergence of material to the wrong channels, causing on one hand shortages, and on the other, excess inventory. We'll have to give the schedule to those (non-constraint) resources, so that they will be restricted from using the available material too early. Schedule for non-constraint resources now has a totally new meaning. It does not tell the resources when to do things, just the opposite. The schedule tells the resources when not to do things; it's a list of "don't do it before . . ."

It wasn't too hard to determine the dates for the activities directly feeding the resource constraints. What about all the activities that feed free orders, orders that don't require even a single activity from any resource constraint? What we said before seems totally applicable; the only thing that we should do differently is to use shipping buffer where before we used resource buffer. The logic seems, even in this case, quite impeccable.

Have we finished? Not yet. What about all the activities on the red lanes, the activities that are needed after the resource constraint has done its part? Shall we use the due-date of the last block as a drum and try to flush out those tasks as fast as we can, or shall we use, as in other cases, the constraint date that they feed, the due-date of the order?

At first sight it might look like a tricky question. We already took care to avoid any conflict between the dates of the resource constraint and the dates of the orders, so why does it matter which one we are going to follow? But examine it a minute longer, and it becomes apparent that removing the conflicts does not necessarily mean that the question does not have meaning.

You see, we have constructed the drum by shifting the blocks backward as well as forward in time. This implies that some blocks might have been scheduled earlier than strictly needed to fulfill their order. They have been scheduled earlier because after that the constraint has to devote its time to other orders. Remember, your client orders are not streaming in beautifully arranged according to the availability of your resource constraint, not to mention seasonal trends and the like. It is more than likely that we'll find blocks scheduled to be done earlier than the due-date of their orders minus the shipping buffer.

Thus, once again, regarding all intermediate operations, the question is: should the non-constraints be instructed to try to flush the inventory as fast as possible, which means to follow the due date of the last block? Or should they be restricted to start working on the units available from the constraint, only according to the instruction derived from the order due-date? It is not a trick, but a real question.

Really? If we follow the peculiar advice that we developed, not to give any schedule to a non-constraint resource, then it doesn't matter which due-date we are going to follow, right? Any material, the minute it is available from the resource constraints, will trigger work at the appropriate resources, so why do we have to worry about it?

Yes, it will do, provided that two different situations are taken care of. The first one is quite obvious—we said that for non-constraints that are using common parts, a schedule must be given. What should we do here? In this situation it's clear which date we must follow. Why do we have to give those resources a schedule to start with? Because we are afraid of stealing, we are afraid that they will use the common material for one purpose when it's actually intended for another. Thus, in the case of resources directly consuming common parts, we'll have to generate a schedule based on the orders' due-dates. No other alternative.

This is one situation. What is the other? Let's hope that it will lead us to the same conclusion, otherwise we are in a jam. The other type of situation that we have to address is when the order is for a product which involves assemblies of many parts, and only one of them needs the participation of a resource constraint. Suppose that the resource constraint, due to capacity limitations, has been scheduled to do its part earlier than required by the order. In that case, the fact that we must do one part ahead of time should not be a valid reason for the production and assembly of all other parts. The client is not willing to accept the order ahead of the required date. What are we going to do with them? It is quite apparent that also, in this case, we have to drive the dates for all other operations according to the order due-date that they are feeding, and not according to the date of the block that feeds them.

Have we covered everything? Let's check. We have covered the operation feeding a resource constraint; we have covered the operations feeding free orders; and we have covered the red lanes, the operations between the blocks and the orders. Have we missed anything? Oh yes, we must address the operations that do not feed a resource constraint and do not feed free orders. Are there any such operations? Yes, and they relate to the situation that we just now analyzed, an assembly that requires only some parts from the resource constraint. What about the operations needed for the other parts? These operations are definitely not on a red lane, and they don't feed a free order.

What's the fuss? We just now said that for those operations we should follow the due date of the corresponding order. Correct, but how are we going to follow it? Shouldn't we use, in this case, the assembly buffer? Yes, of course. First we should derive the date for the assembly by subtracting the shipping buffer from the corresponding order due-date. But this will not be enough; we have to guarantee that all non-constraint parts arrive before the parts which come from the resource constraint. Thus, we'll have to further subtract, from the calculated date of the assembly, the time of the assembly buffer. The resulting date is the one that we use for all these activities, in particular the material release of the non-constraint parts.

Figure 16 shows the case of one order for a product that involves more than one level of assembly and more than one operation done by a resource constraint. The order due-date and the dates of the blocks are already dictated by the drum step; all other dates are derived according to what we said so far. Please verify.

In all the cases we have examined so far, the answer was the same: the schedule of an action should be derived according to the constraint date the operation feeds. Such lovely symmetry, it must be valid. Yes, but up to a point. What we have described so far is the manual drum-buffer-rope procedure, a procedure that has proven its validity in so many real-life implementations. Unfortunately, it is far from being sufficient for our purpose. We don't want just a schedule, our main purpose is the identification of all the company's constraints.

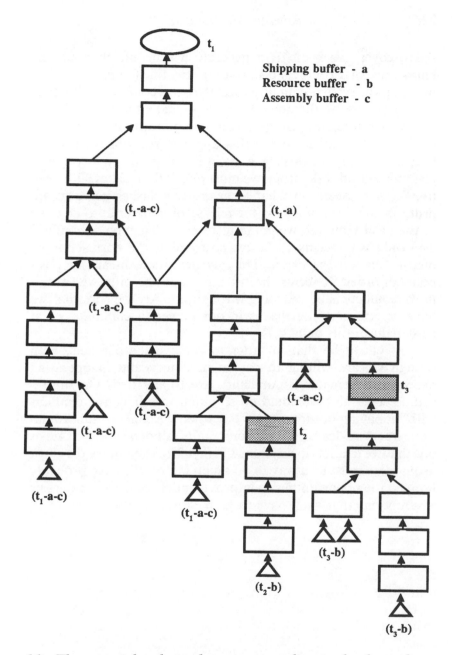

Shipping buffer - a
Resource buffer - b
Assembly buffer - c

16 The materials release dates are according to the drum dates and sizes of the time buffers.

Moreover, we wanted to generate a schedule without any known internal conflicts between the identified constraints. An information system cannot afford that the conflicts will be removed mainly by the floor personnel—that's too late.

You see, following the procedure that we outlined, in what form will the clashes with reality appear? Yes, this is the question that should, at this stage, be in front of our eyes. We have just finished subordination; we must check for clashes with reality. So, once again, in what form are the clashes going to appear? In the form of asking for release of a material to be done in the past! How are we going to resolve that type of conflict? The only way seems to be by postponing the corresponding instructions on the drum. This, by definition, means to postpone an order. It seems that at this stage the only way to remove conflicts is by reducing throughput. Are we sure that we have done everything that is in our power to eliminate, or at least reduce, this damage?

How can it be that in order to remove the conflicts, even though we are willing to pay in inventory and in operating expense, it seems as if our hands are totally tied? On the resource constraint we could do so much to relieve the conflicts without paying in throughput, but when we come to subordination, when we deal with non-constraints, all of a sudden it turns out that we cannot do anything? Fishy. No, even more than just fishy; there must be a way to do much better. We have probably lumped the opportunities to improve under some parameters or assumptions that we'll have to go back and undo.

35. *Subordinating while considering non-constraints' capacity—the conceptual approach*

Where can we start to look for the key to this intolerable situation? Let's view it carefully. Let's try to gather all the open points, all the ones that we feel were somehow left in an unsatisfactory position.

We were supposed to identify the system's constraints. We said, over and over again, that there is probably more than just one resource constraint, maybe another bottleneck or at least a resource that doesn't have enough protective capacity. We said that we are going to catch them, one by one like sitting ducks, through the cycle of identify, exploit, subordinate. Here we are, at the end of subordination, with a whole bunch of conflicts, but they are conflicts with time, with the unrealistic need to do things in the past. We cannot use these conflicts for the identification of the next resource constraint; they are not conflicts of load versus availability of capacity.

Why are we surprised? We didn't consider capacity at all in the subordination stage. But how could we? Aren't we supposed to ignore capacity at this stage? Isn't considering capacity something that we do only when we know that it is lacking? Probably not.

The entire subordination process seems to revolve around

subtracting the various buffers from the dates already set by the drum. The only additional data that we use are the length of the buffers. Does capacity have anything to do with the length of the buffers? Bingo! This seems to be the key question. We have stepped on another point that was left open. Do you remember that when we discussed the things that determine the length of a buffer, we said that capacity is one of the dominant factors? What did we call it? Non-instant availability of resources, or something like that. Which resources did we talk about? The non-constraint resources. Yes, this is definitely the key to our problem. It all fits together.

First, let's refresh our memory. It's unfair to demand more than a vague recollection about something with a frightening name like "non-instant availability of resources." What was the issue here? Oh yes, we discussed the fact that the actual process time is a very small contributor to the overall lead time. Now it starts to come back. We said that even though we might have, on the average, more than enough capacity, when work arrives at the resource it might have to wait in the queue, because the resource might be occupied with some other necessary work.

Well, what can we do about it? Probably quite a lot. We have all the data we want. Maybe it is possible to get a good handle on when these temporary loads are going to occur. If we actually can do this and take it into account, maybe we will be able to take capacity into account while we subordinate. Let's try to figure out how we can actually do it. What do we have to lose; we are already in a deep ditch, anyhow.

Nothing prevents us now from calculating the daily loads for each non-constraint resource. It is quite a straightforward calculation, just like what MRP has done for years. We do know the resource availability on a daily basis, since we have the calendars. Dividing one list by the other will give us a clear indication of when and where the overloads are going to occur. Yes, it will be just an approximation; we know that work will tend to arrive later, mainly due to these same overloads, but certainly it is going to be a very valid and useful approximation.

Useful? In what way? What are we actually going to do with

the resulting picture, which will probably resemble the Manhattan skyline? And please, don't tell me that it's going to provide us with better insight! As long as the computer is involved, better insight is synonymous with stating, "We really don't know what to do with it." What is a computer going to do with better insight?

Ha ha, you want to dump the ball into the user's lap. Are you going to tell me that the user should now put the mountains into the valleys? How is the user going to perform this miracle? MRP tried to do it under the "sophisticated" title of a "closed loop." Show me even one implementation that has succeeded in getting out of that loop. Don't you realize that shifting back a mountain of load on one resource necessitates a corresponding shift on other resources? They do feed each other. You may take care of one mountain, but you probably create other mountains, maybe bigger ones, on other resources. Everybody knows that this "closed loop" is an "endless loop"; this iterative process simply doesn't converge.

OK, we've released some steam, but it is quite clear that a good solution is hidden somewhere in this area, so let's go and find it . . . but slowly, it's definitely hidden deep inside a minefield.

Consider one such overload peak on one resource. It's apparent that we cannot leave it there; we cannot make a resource work more than 100% of its capability. Come on, we are not dealing with a crooked system of norms and premiums, where everybody regularly performs at 130%; we are dealing with our best estimations. So, what are we going to do about this peak load? Please don't even dare to think about overtime. Don't forget that we are dealing with non-constraint resources. Should we use overtime to increase capacity on resources that already have more than enough? What a ridiculous thought!

It's obvious that we have to try to move the peak into a nearby valley. There must be enough valleys, as long as we are dealing with a non-constraint. No, we shouldn't search for a valley forward in time; what are we going to do with that valley? Moving our peak in that direction means postponing orders, jeopardizing throughput. We should move the peak to the past, backward in time.

Wait; if we touch the peak, moving it in either direction, won't we need to move the loads on other feeding resources as well?

Yes, certainly, but what's the big deal? From what we said so far, we can logically conclude the following: we must push the mountains into the past, and we must do so in a way that guarantees that the resulting loads can be done on all resources. Thus, it is crystal clear that we shouldn't be looking for the load profiles after we've done the entire schedule. This is much too late.

Rather, in constructing the schedule, we must be very careful to move consistently backward in time. No operation should be scheduled at a particular date until all other operations that need to be scheduled at a latter date have been already taken care of. That's the only way we can guarantee that if we shovel a peak load to an earlier date, its feeding operations are going to land on a valley rather than on an even higher mountain. It also means that we have to collect the load data for each resource and do the appropriate shoveling, not after, but while, constructing the schedule for the non-constraints.

You make it sound so simple. Not that I fully understand what you are saying, but tell me, hasn't MRP scheduling always been backward in time? If you are right, what's the big deal for MRP to compute the loads while scheduling, rather than to complete the scheduling task first and only then do the load calculations? Why haven't they done the same thing? No, probably it's not so simple. Probably it's much more complicated than you are suggesting . . . and thus I suspect that it's also probably very wrong.

Fine, let's examine it in detail. Anyhow, we still have to convert it into a workable procedure; this was just an outline. But before we do just that, tell me, why do you claim that MRP is backward scheduling? Yes, I too am aware that everybody thinks so, but that doesn't make it true. The way I understand what MRP is doing, and let me choose one of the simplest procedures (anyhow, they all lead to exactly the same end answer)—the way that MRP is moving on the time axis is . . . Maybe I'd better use an example.

Imagine that the entire product structure is only one product having one assembly of two parts. For this product we have many orders with different due-dates. How will MRP move on the time axis when it schedules this company?

It must start from the earliest order, otherwise MRP will have problems allocating the existing stocks. Not clear? OK. Suppose that MRP started with the latest order—remember, MRP is allocating the WIP stocks while doing the scheduling. Try to imagine the users' response when they find out that the stocks they have produced for an urgent order have all of a sudden been assigned to an order that has to be fulfilled a month from now. On top of this, the dumb computer is now asking them to hurry up and expedite the production of the same stocks!

So MRP starts with the earliest order. Please, put your finger at the appropriate place on the time axis—on this order's due-date. Now, MRP starts to explode the product structure. In doing so it moves backward in time. Please move your finger accordingly. It first reaches the assembly. Where to go from here? It must choose one of the two legs, one of the two parts that have to be produced. Picking one of them, it will continue to dive down this leg, and your finger continues moving to the left. So far we are moving backward in time, no problem. MRP reaches the material and deals with it; what's next? We still have another part to schedule, so it goes to the assembly and starts to dive down the second leg. Wait, not so fast! What should your finger do? Moving back to the assembly means moving forward in time, and then diving down the second leg means moving again backward in time. Your finger has made a lovely zig-zag on the time axis. We've now finished this order, now what?

Why don't we tango? Going to the next order means moving your finger further to the right. Dive through one part—now to the left, please. Now to assembly—to the right again; to the second part—to the left; to the next order—even further to the right . . . and so on. This is what we call backward in time? In my eyes it resembles a zig-zag in time, with a strong tendency to continually move forward in time.

Enough of these fairy tales. MRP is backward scheduling? Let's be serious. How can we devise a procedure that will consistently go backward in time, while bulldozing the overloads?

36. *Dynamic time buffers and protective capacity*

Going consistently backward in time dictates that we'll have to start with the latest thing that we are going to do. If we start at any other point, we'll eventually be forced to go forward. The latest thing is, no doubt, the latest order. Or, being more precise, the latest order that is earlier than the horizon date plus a shipping buffer. Do you agree?

No, that is not the place to start. If we do it that way, the stocks are going to be allocated to the latest orders. We need to start by allocating the stocks.

Didn't we already do this when we generated the blocks for the drum? Yes, but then we only allocated the stocks that resided on the red lanes. At that stage there was no need to allocate more than this portion, and there was no point in allocating the stocks residing in the other portion. Remember that we are allocating according to the orders' due-dates—first come, first served. When we authorized the drum, we very likely changed some order due-dates, and thus, now is the time to complete the allocation.

This won't take a long time. Since all relevant data resides in on-line memory, such steps can be done at breath-taking speed. If we want to continue to procrastinate, we'll have to come up with better, "longer" ideas.

What about the buffer length? This looks like a juicy one. What about it?

We said that one of the dominant reasons for the task's lead-time was non-instant availability of non-constraint resources. We are going to take this into account now. Won't it change the user's initial choice of the appropriate length of the various buffers? Shouldn't we discuss it before we start to subordinate? Remember, the subordination process is heavily based on the length of the buffers.

You certainly have a point. What is really the meaning of shoveling a peak load into an earlier valley? In less colorful words, it simply means that an action that we would like to schedule at a certain date will, due to capacity considerations, have to be scheduled at an earlier date. Is it the only activity whose date is impacted? No, all activities that feed it have to be moved accordingly, including, of course, the release date of the appropriate material. The end result of considering overload peaks is to release materials earlier than the date dictated by the buffer length. It is equivalent to increasing the original length of the buffer for just these activities.

Yes, this mechanism is going to quite accurately consider the impact that non-instant availability has on the task's lead-time. Let's try to digest this pleasant surprise. One of the most diffi-cult problems that we have struggled with in the past was how to estimate individual queue times. Everyone who has tried to implement MRP knows that determining queue times is a con-stant struggle between production and material personnel.

The constant fire-fighting and priority shuffling suggests that queue times have been underestimated. The pressure to reduce the overall lead-time is forcing us to recognize that in aggrega-tion they were overestimated. In some defense industries we'll find that the queue times are set at one week for each operation and are unrelated to the actual length of the activity. Neverthe-less, shortages at assembly are taken almost as a *fait accompli.* In spite of constant debates, everybody involved knows too well that the queue time estimations at a given work center are just wild guesses. In design engineering the situation is even worse.

There queue times are lumped with execution times, leading to a total mistrust of any time estimations.

It's no wonder. Queue times are not a function of the individual tasks to be done, they are mainly a function of the load which is placed on the resource. Orders do not arrive in an even stream, and the mix of orders can change continuously. Consequently, the load placed on each type of resource can fluctuate considerably—for two days a particular resource works frantically, the next day it has almost nothing to do. Trying to assign a number for the queue time is an attempt to represent this dynamic entity by an imaginary "average queue time." Trying to portray a sharply fluctuating entity with a number that represents an average can only lead to very unsatisfactory results.

In using time buffers rather than individual queue times, we no doubt improve considerably. The usual concept of queue time is trying to make the averaging on the resource level—how much time, on the average, does a task have to wait in front of that resource. This doesn't help. Spare capacity tomorrow doesn't help me today, and spare capacity yesterday, when the material hadn't arrived, does not help me today. But making the averaging on the task level—using the concept of time buffers and the triggering of expediting—definitely helps.

What we propose here seems to be the next improvement step. We can predict, quite reliably, the expected fluctuations in load. They are dictated by the given changes in the market constraints modified by the internal constraints. What we're suggesting is timing the release of materials according to the expected load fluctuations. This will definitely reduce the time material has to wait in front of a resource, and thus significantly reduce the overall lead-time.

We just wanted a mechanism to identify the company's constraints. We got, as a side benefit, a further significant decrease in inventory. That is definitely a sign we are heading in the right direction.

Yes, the original estimates of the time buffers will have to be reduced considerably. What we have to give to our information system as the buffer's length is not the estimate of the total lead-time but something smaller. We have to estimate only the impact that "pure Murphy" has on the lead time; we can ignore the impact of non-instant availability. This latter portion is going to be taken care of by the system itself, on a case-by-case basis. What we actually have to supply to the information system is the "fixed" portion of the time buffer. The system has to determine the variable portion. We basically are going to use DYNAMIC BUFFERING.

A side note. We actually should go back and rewrite the entire explanation of the subordination process, using the terms "fixed portion" and "variable portion." Luckily, it turns out that we can safely continue without creating any confusion. Where we referred to the time buffer, it should be understood that we were referring to just the fixed portion of the time buffer.

Of course, the original estimates of the time-buffer length are going to be constantly modified by "buffer management," but how do we get the initial estimate? We have to start some place, and nobody yet has the experience of evaluating just a portion of the lead time—the one stemming from pure Murphy. My advice at this stage depends on the level of actual experience the user has in implementing the time buffers. If you already have a manual implementation of drum-buffer-rope, cut the buffer length in half. Otherwise estimate the current average lead-time of the tasks and divide it by five. This will provide a nice starting point.

The last reason for procrastinating turned out to be extremely fruitful; maybe we should find another one. As a matter of fact we have. Not exactly an idea, but a very troubling question.

You see, this leveling of the peaks leads to quite lengthy time periods where a resource will be fully loaded. Basically, a resource may be scheduled to work 100% of its available capacity for many days. During this time interval it is obvious that this resource will not have any protective capacity; all its available capacity is dedicated to production. For how long, for how many days, are we going to let a non-constraint go without any protective capacity before admitting that we have a problem?

What a question—but you are right, we have to address this issue. Let's see . . . A resource needs to have protective capacity in order to restore the damage caused by disturbances, not just at that resource, but at all the activities feeding it. What type of damage are we talking about in this case? Basically, the damage of exposing the constraints.

The constraint is protected, at any given point in time, only by the content of the "material" residing in the buffer-origin. Remember, this does not have to be physical inventory; in the case of a market constraint it can take the form of early shipments; in the case of engineering it might be a drawing or even required data. We have stressed that protection is not provided by just any inventory; it must be the right inventory, the "materials" that are scheduled to be consumed by the constraint.

Let's try now to create the following mental picture. Forget the subject of temporary overloads; those we are taking care of separately, here we are dealing with regular disturbances. Consider a task that is scheduled to be done by a constraint sometime between now and a time buffer from now. If this task does not now reside in the buffer-origin, let's call it a "hole in the buffer-origin."

Let's try to track a typical journey of such a hole. Suppose that now there is a time buffer before a task's scheduled due-date on the drum—a hole starts to penetrate into the buffer origin. As time goes by, and our task does not arrive, the hole continues to penetrate deeper and deeper into the buffer-origin. It soon crosses the tracking zone and enters the expediting zone. If it remains missing, the constraint will have to deviate from plan. Damage to the throughput occurs.

Bearing this picture in mind, let's turn back to the issue of protective capacity. Examine a non-constraint resource working 100% on a particular day. On that day this resource does not have any protective capacity, which means that due to disturbances, tasks will (on average) be delayed from reaching the buffer-origin. Holes penetrate into the buffer origin. By how much? Well, it depends. On what? It must depend on the level of protective capacity the resource needed and on the length of the buffer.

How can we get a firmer handle on this issue? Maybe we should try to use some numbers. Suppose a resource needs 5% protective capacity. This means that 5 percent of its time must be free to help the company recover from the impact of disturbances. In other words, it means that 5% protective capacity is needed so that the resource will not "contribute" to the progression of holes in the buffer-origins that it feeds. If the resource has no protective capacity for one day, the holes are going to progress an additional 5% of a day into the buffer-origin. On the average, of course. We are not dealing with deterministic events but with statistical ones, with disturbances.

Now the answer is obvious. Each consecutive day the resource is fully loaded, the hole progresses by the fraction of a day that is equal to the percentage presentation of the needed protective capacity. How many consecutive days can we allow a non-constraint resource to be fully utilized? We have to decide how far we are going to allow the holes to penetrate before we consider it a problem. Let's decide on half the buffer; more than that is like playing Russian roulette with five bullets.

This means that when we subordinate, we'll have to be careful that a resource is not running for too long before we enforce unscheduled time on it. Basically, we must constantly track what the loading of every resource is going to do to our imaginary holes. But since we understand the relationship of protective capacity and buffer length, this becomes relatively simple programming work.

Anything else?

37. *Some residual issues*

Now can we start to construct the subordination procedure? Not yet; we still have several points that should be hammered out.

Talking about shoveling peaks backward in time, how are we going to treat a peak created by an activity on a red lane? Moving that activity to an early date will necessitate a respective move of a block, of an activity done by the constraint itself. I thought that subordinate meant follow, not modify.

Fine, it's apparent that peaks created by an activity on the red lane, or "red-lane peaks" for short, need special attention.

First we have to check to see if this situation actually exists for our red-lane peak; in other words, if shoveling the peak creates the necessity to move the corresponding block. This will occur only when there is no "slack," when the date of the block is not earlier than the date of the order minus the shipping buffer. As we said, or at least indicated earlier, this is not always the case. Sometimes the block is placed much earlier, due to a resource-constraint peak. Other times, more than one block is generated by the same order, and if the due-date of the order is reset as a result of a red block, all other blocks have "slack."

If there is sufficient slack, we can treat the red-lane peak like any other peak. If there isn't, we'll have to deal with the peak itself.

First, let's remember that in such extreme cases we are willing to be satisfied with only half the buffer. Leaving the peak as is means that this task will generate a hole in the buffer-origin; every hour above the available capacity (on the date of the peak) will cause the hole to penetrate another hour into the buffer-origin. Thus the maximum peak hours that we can live with are dictated by the length of the buffer. This is actually equivalent to shoveling forward, sacrificing protection.

Suppose we use this latitude to its maximum, and we still have a hole. Now let's use the permission for overtime, if it's available. If this won't help, let's call the user. The user will have to choose between authorizing additional overtime—the system must tell how much is still needed; or off-loading the task to another resource—the system must tell what is the minimum quantity that must be off-loaded; or postponing the order —the system must tell to what date. Any other possibilities? Yes, the user may know that the problem occurred because of erroneous data, and might elect to instruct the system to ignore the peak and carry on.

And what happens if it is a real problem? What can the user do if none of the above possibilities are realistic? Then it looks as if we have an additional constraint, doesn't it? The resource exhibiting this peak should be declared a constraint, and the system should abandon any effort to continue at this stage. The intermediate target is achieved—we identified an additional constraint. The system must turn to the next step of resolving the conflicts between the already identified constraints.

Sounds OK to me. Let's move to the next open point. I would like to question how we take into account the time required to actually perform an operation. I understand that we are taking into account the impact the process times have on the overall lead-time, through the load they place on the resources. I also understand, and agree, that the direct contribution of process time is quite small—but still, process times do make some contribution. We have all the necessary data, why shouldn't we take this direct contribution into account?

Let's see. What you suggest is to calculate, for each operation, the time to do a batch, by multiplying the process time per unit by the number of units required, adding the set-up time, and then summing the results along the sequence of operations needed to do the task. Look what will happen if we follow your suggestion.

Suppose that we are dealing with an industrial line. Assume that the line contains ten different work centers, and that the time to process a unit at a work center ranges from less than a minute to a maximum of two minutes. Now take a case where the order is for several hundred units. If we follow your suggestion, what will we get? Since the process time of the entire order at each work center is about a day, we'll get the impression that even if there are no disturbances, it will take about a week to complete the order. Ridiculous; we all know that it will only take about one day.

If we take into account the time to do an entire batch at each operation, we ignore the possibility of overlapping the batches between different operations. As in a line, even though it takes a day to complete the order at one work center, it doesn't preclude starting the work at the next work center immediately after the first unit is completed. You see, if we ask what is the direct contribution of process times, it's even smaller than we thought. If no problem of resource availability exists, as in a line, and Murphy does not exist, then the time to complete the order is almost equal to the time required to complete the order at just one work center—the one having the longest process time. If you want to be even more precise, the time to complete the order is equal to the time it takes to do the order at the longest operation plus the summation of the time it takes to do one single unit at all other operations. This is always ridiculously small compared to non-instant availability and Murphy. Why should we bother to calculate it just because the data is available?

Whatever you said sounds right, but this assumes the ability to overlap activities throughout all the operations required to perform the task. This is not always possible. I'm not referring to environments where it's definitely possible, but forbidden due to some ridiculous policies hiding behind the false pretense of better control. No, in those environments the policy constraints should be elevated. I'm referring to situations where overlapping is impractical because of technical limitations. Take for example a batch-type oven, where once the batch enters the oven, and the door is closed, all units in the batch have to wait until the process is completed and the door is opened again. Transportation is another case where we simply cannot dedicate a van for each single unit. In cases where the entire batch is processed together, there is no technical possibility for overlapping.

Thus, the direct contribution of the actual process time to the overall lead-time is the time to process the batch on the longest operation, plus the time required to process the batch at operations that cannot be overlapped, plus the time to process one unit at all other operations. We do have all the required data; why won't we use it?

If you insist. Anything else, or can we at last start to build the subordination mechanism?

One last question, if you still have any patience left. In the subordination step, should we try to save set-up time?

Why should we? What is the purpose of saving set-up? What are we actually saving here? Not money, but time. Do we have any use for this time? Will it help us to increase throughput? The throughput is dictated by the organization's constraints, and we are dealing here with non-constraints only. If, because of set-up time, a rcsource does not have enough capacity, we declare it as a constraint and treat the set-up requirements accordingly. So why should we bother with set-up in the subordination step?

Throughput is not the only way our bottom line is affected. Inventory and operating expense should also be considered, even though to a lesser extent. Let's see if they will cause us to consider set-up savings even in the subordination step.

Whenever we have to make an effort to save set-up, it means that we have to "jump" a batch that otherwise would be done in the more remote future. Saving set-ups increases inventories;

inventory considerations will just direct us away from attempts to save set-up.

Unless, of course, the set-up contribution is so large that it creates a constraint. If this is the case, we have to pay in inventory to protect that constraint against disruptions. Let's decide to do two things. The first is to try and save set-up before we declare a second resource constraint. Remember that in identifying the first resource constraint we used the minimum amount of set-up time (one set-up per part-number/operation and not per order), which is equivalent to the maximum possible set-up savings.

When do we try to identify an additional resource constraint? When the subordination step is completed and we have a peak of load that we cannot shovel into the past. At this stage we'll examine all the batches in the peak and get all the set-up savings. I doubt if it will amount to much, but it will probably help to reduce the amount of off-load and overtime that would otherwise be needed to resolve the peak without declaring it a resource constraint.

There is something more we can do. If set-up considerations are important in our environment, then very early on we are going to identify a resource constraint that will require a lot of "gluing" of its blocks. If in subordination we treat a string of glued blocks as one block, rather than following the original individual blocks, we will save a lot of set-up on all the feeding resources. In this case, we have already paid most of the inventory penalty, because the drum had to "jump" blocks. The additional penalty of treating the glued blocks as one is relatively small, and the chance to help is relatively big.

What about saving set-up time because of operating expense considerations? This is starting to go too far. The only effective way to impact operating expense is by reducing the need for overtime. Where do we permit overtime? On the drum, where we try to save set-up anyhow; on the peak loads shoveled into the first day, where once again we already decided to try to save set-up time; and on red-lane peaks. In the latter case we cannot, anyhow, move the batch to the past. So what are we actually talking about?

Enough is enough. Let's construct the procedure that will allow the subordination to properly take into account the capacity of non-constraint resources.

38. *The details of the subordination procedure*

Basically, all the ingredients necessary to construct the subordination procedure are already in our possession; some, I suspect, are overly polished. Now, we just have to mold them together. Unfortunately, after all the possible difficulties have been addressed, describing a procedure becomes very technical. Anybody that is not a system freak can leave now and return after this chapter, unless of course you want to fall asleep.

The most important guideline is to be very consistent in moving only backward in time. This means that before the system assigns an operation to a specific date, it must make sure that all operations that should be assigned to a later date have already been dealt with. We would hate to leave anything unattended behind, since any attempt to go back and pick up a "leftover" is a violation of our decision to consistently go backward in time.

This innocent paragraph, which almost looks redundant, is actually dictating the entire procedure.

First of all, it's now obvious that when going backward in time, the system must be very conscious of the date it is currently dealing with. From now on, let's refer to this date as the "current date."

Second, the almost hysterical warning against leaving anything behind simply tells us that we don't want to move from the current date without a very good reason. This immediately raises the question of what things will cause us to move on the time axis? If we consider the negligible impact that the process time of each operation has on the task's lead time, then each operation will cause us to move in time. This, on the face of it, is an obvious case of over-sophistication—considering something that complicates things appreciably, but that doesn't have any real-life impact.

Thus, we have to decide on an interval of time to represent the maximum sensitivity of the system. Anything that is less than this interval should be ignored as a reason to move the current date. Since the order due-dates are usually given without specifying a particular hour, it seems reasonable that as far as movements backward in time are concerned, we should choose one day as the unit of maximum sensitivity.

This leaves three different categories that will necessitate a move in time. The first category is the drum. Whenever we reach an activity of the drum, we must consider its date, which might be different from the current date.

The second category is the buffers. Whenever we dive down from an order, or from an operation done by a resource constraint, or from a red-lane operation to a regular operation, we must provide for the corresponding time buffer.

The third category is peaks of overload. Shoveling a peak might mean to assign the corresponding operations to an earlier date. To handle this category we'll have to choose a minimum unit of time, since load is not defined at a point, but rather at an interval. Once again, we need a unit of time we regard as significant. Why don't we stick with the choice that we already made —a day.

As we go down the product's structure, each time that we encounter one of these three categories, we have to mark where we are, so we can return to that point, but we shouldn't continue to dive. As the subordination process continues, we'll probably have to keep more such reminders, so why don't we arrange them into an ordered "reminder list." At the top of the list will be the reminder closest to the current date and at the bottom the one that is closest to the present. Remember, we are moving backward in time; everything is upside down.

When we start, our reminder list is not empty. It should contain the entire drum—the due-dates of the orders and the ending time of the resource constraints' blocks. We also know that along the subordination process, due to the second and third categories, many more new "reminders" are going to be added to our list.

Now let's begin the subordination process. Let's take the highest entry on the list and start to dive from it. The highest on the list is, most likely, an order, and we should dive from it into the feeding operations (we might find more than one, since the order might be for a basket of products). But first we have to subtract the shipping buffer. This will necessitate moving backward. We cannot do it right now because there might be other orders with the same current date. Thus we're just going to identify the operations that directly feed the order and put the corresponding notes on our reminder list.

Whenever we add a new member to the reminder list, the position it gets on the list will be based on the date assigned to it. Remember any date that is before the present should be set to be equal to the date of the present; there is no point in giving instructions for the past. Thus, in this case the assigned date is the order date minus the shipping buffer, or the present date, whichever is bigger. Now that we have dealt with this order, we can erase it from the reminder list and move to the next candidate.

Continuing to follow those steps will cause us, eventually, to pick an operation, not an order, from the list. We then have to deal with the operation itself. We'll have to calculate the load that it represents and adjust accordingly the current available capacity of the resource which is supposed to perform that operation.

If the additional load is more than the available capacity, we'll have to put the surplus into the resource's "left-over load" entry. Since the available current capacity is exhausted, no other operations needing this resource can be scheduled on the current date. An exception to the above is when the current date reaches the present date; in this case all loads are added to the first day since there is no possibility for left-over load.

None of this will affect the current date, and thus we can continue to dive down, recording every assembly we pass through, until we encounter one of three different situations.

The first one is probably the most common; we simply reached a material. In this case we will have to jump back to the nearest higher assembly—remember no movement in time has yet occurred—and dive down additional legs if they exist. If no assembly is marked, we can return to our reminder list.

The second situation occurs when in our diving we reach an operation of the drum. We do not deal with this operation, it has already been taken care of. We simply have to return to the highest assembly (if it exists) or to the reminder list.

The third situation occurs when we try to adjust the availability of the corresponding resource, and we find that its current availability is already zero. In this case we have to go back to the reminder list, since dealing with this operation means going back in time. The proper place on this list will be determined by the amount of the left-over load of the corresponding resource.

This technique will force us to jump like a grasshopper from one product structure location to another, but since all the data resides in memory it does not represent a technical problem. The entire process is done using only on-line memory, because there is no need to store the resulting schedule, for either the release of material or for any other operation.

Remember, at this stage we are not sure whether or not we are going to find an additional constraint, so why should we waste a lot of time recording the results on the disk. An additional constraint will necessitate, by definition, a change in subordination, and thus it is very likely that the current schedule will not be the final one. When no conflict has been observed at the end of subordination, we will repeat the entire last round of subordination and write the schedule to the disk. It is far more economic to "waste" a subordination cycle than to "waste" writing on the disk.

We'll continue to follow this basic process and use the guidelines developed in the last two chapters to deal with the special cases. The finer technical details are awfully boring and can be found in the appropriate manual, so why should we suffer through them; it's definitely not going to teach us anything new.

The system will continue to grind until we exhaust the reminder list. This concludes this round of subordination. We now have to find how we should check for any resulting conflicts.

39. *Identifying the next constraint, and looping back*

Most likely, the subordination stage has left us with some resources that are overloaded on the first day. Actually, this is not an accurate enough description. When there is still an unidentified resource constraint, shoveling the peaks backward in time creates not just overloads on the first day, it creates mountains of overloads, and not on just one resource. Not all the resources that exhibit impressive peaks are constraints. Considering the capacity limitations of one resource will reduce the load on all others. How should we choose the next constraint?

The severity of the limitations imposed on the company by determining the lack of sufficient capacity is not fully shown by the amount of hours that are missing. Consider for example, one resource that is lacking 100 hours (the number of load hours accumulated on the first day minus the resource availability) and another which is missing only 50 hours. We should not rush to conclude that our next choice is the first resource. It might be that the smallest buffer that the first resource precedes has a length of 200 hours, while for the second resource the buffer length is only 20 hours. In this case it is obvious that the second resource presents a much bigger limitation.

This means that the system should first try to minimize the overload by using set-up savings, permitted overtime, and half-buffer, forward shoveling. But then, we should consider the remaining overload according to the limitation it imposes on the overall operation—which means according to the magnitude of the resulting damage to the company, not the number of hours still missing.

The expected damage can be best illustrated by displaying the overloads in units of the depth of expected penetration of the resulting holes, expressed in buffer length. For example, an overload of three means that the overload will cause holes to penetrate into the buffer origin beyond the danger limit (remember we have already used half the protection) to a distance equal to three times the length of the buffer.

Since the user can still take steps to overcome an overload, before declaring an additional constraint, the list of all resources having a first day peak should be displayed. The system should sort the list according to the depth of penetration, but still display the hours of overload.

This last piece of data is still important, since it helps the users to decide whether or not there is a need to declare another constraint. Remember, we are not in a rush to declare another constraint, since each additional constraint means the need for additional protection and thus an increase in inventory. On the other hand, if we'll declare a resource as a constraint anyhow, there is no point relaxing the first day overload on that resource as well as all other non-constraint resources.

This last point might need additional clarification. Suppose a resource needs 50 percent protective capacity. This protective capacity protects not the resource itself but the feasibility of exploiting the system's constraints. Thus the minute this resource is recognized as a constraint, all its protective capacity is freed for exploitation. We pay with the need to increase protection in other portions of the system, but we are getting more capacity here. As a result, all attempts to increase the resource capacity by overtime and off-load will be regarded as null and void the minute that the resource itself is declared as a constraint. The conclusion is that once it is obvious we cannot eliminate the first-day peak, then there is no point in trying to just minimize it.

The major manual weapon the user has at this stage is not overtime but off-loading to other resources. Thus the list of candidate batches to be off-loaded for each resource must be ready for display upon request.

Suppose that in spite of all efforts, another resource constraint is identified; how should we treat it? The method is now much better understood. Concentrating on this resource, we should ask ourselves what should it do if no internal limitation existed. In other words, let's construct the "ruins" picture for that resource. Let's take the drum as given, the shipping buffer lengths as given, but only half the resource buffer (this was always the rule) when one resource constraint operation is feeding another. We compute what (the block) and when (the ending time of the block) this new constraint has to perform, assuming infinite availability.

Now let's start to consider the availability of this resource and check for conflicts. We have to be a little bit more careful in this stage and check for conflicts with the instructions of the current drum. Previously we didn't have to do this because there was no possibility of conflicts, since the drum was composed only of the due-dates of the orders. But here the situation is different, since the current drum includes instructions for another resource constraint.

To represent the interrelations between blocks of the first resource constraint (old blocks) and blocks of the second resource constraint (new blocks), let's use again the concept of rods, but in this case we will need to define "time rods."

If a new block is feeding, directly or indirectly, an old block, the new block must be finished at least half a buffer before the date of the old block. Thus let's attach to the new block an imaginary "time rod." This particular time rod is equal to the length of half a resource buffer, and it is sensitive to the date of the old block. This date is for our "time rod" what an iron wall is for a regular rod. To accurately describe the freedom allowed for the movement in time of our new block, we'll have to attach the time rod to the right of the new block. Let's refer to such blocks as F blocks (F to symbolize a block with a rod pointing FORWARD in time).

For a new block fed by an old block, let's attach a time rod to the left of the block. Everything else stays the same; the length is still half the resource buffer, and the iron-wall date is the date of the old block. Let's refer to such blocks as B blocks (a rod pointing BACKWARD in time).

As we said, considering the availability of the new constraint may expose conflicts with the date established for the old resource constraint. The time rods will help in clarifying these possible conflicts.

The first possible conflict is a rare one. It might occur when the "old" resource constraint has blocks with "rods." Just as a reminder, rods are attached to blocks when one block feeds, through other operations, another block done by the same constraint. Try to imagine that one of the intermediate operations is done by the second resource constraint. If there is no slack between the "old" blocks, there will be no room for the additional buffer that is now required by the "new" block. In other words, whenever we have a new block that has backward AND forward time rods (a BF block), we may run into a conflict with the old drum.

Even if there were slack, we might still run into problems. It is quite obvious that we have very limited freedom to place the BF blocks, and there might be more than one competing on the same time interval. Thus, when we consider the fact that only a finite number of units are available from the new resource constraint, let's use a refined bulldozer.

In coming to deal with the new constraint "ruins," our refined bulldozer lifts all the blocks up in the air and initially deals only with the BF blocks. As the bulldozer levels the BF blocks, it might face the need to move a block in violation of a time rod. Here we have a conflict that can be resolved only in one of two ways. Either the new block is off-loaded from the new resource constraint, or the initial drum is modified. The choice is not a system choice but a user choice.

Once the BF blocks are dealt with, the bulldozer has to level the F blocks, treating the BF blocks as unmovable rocks. Here we might find the bulldozer pushing F blocks beyond the present date, in clear violation of reality. Once again, the only way to resolve the conflicts is through off-loading or modifying the previous drum.

If we have to modify the original drum, we'll do it at this stage. All old blocks that participate in the violations will now turn into B blocks, acquiring time rods that will ensure minimum push to the future. The process has started again. We forget the existence of the second resource constraint; it left its mark through the attachment of the time rods to the old constraint's blocks. We repeat the exploitation, subordination, and choosing of the new resource constraint.

Shouldn't we be afraid that we will have to go through this cycle forever and ever? Not at all. The new constraint always places limitations in one direction on the old constraint. Overall, this process forces a movement of the load to the future and thus relaxes the possibility of conflict within the specified horizon. The nature of this iterative process is such that it must converge, and fast.

If no violation of the previous resource constraints has occurred, we still have to deal with violations of available capacity of the current constraint and with the conflicts with the market demands. Thus the system should repeat the process with the B blocks and the free blocks. Here there is no need to check; there is no possible way for a conflict with the old resource constraint. The same treatment of red blocks is done. Then subordination takes place when the starting point of the reminder list contains the blocks of all constraints.

The system repeats the process until all the overloads on the first day are resolved, all constraints have been identified, exploited, and subordinated to, and no known conflicts have been left for the floor personnel to resolve. It seems as if we actually have made it.

But wait; how many constraints will be found in this way? If not mistaken, we have proven that if chain has more than one weak link, it will be very quickly torn by reality. Or in a less metaphoric way, we should not allow interactive resource constraints. The mere fact that we consider cases where one resource constraint has a "rod" pointing to another resource constraint, clearly indicates that we allow for interactive constraints. Should we?

Almost any attempt to use the information system to analyze a real company revealed that this type of situation does exist in reality. Yes, in all cases, due-date performance was quite horrible and expediting seemed to be the way by which the companies were run, but these companies do survive. On the other hand, checking the logic that has led us to the warning against interactive constraints does not reveal any logical flow. The only possible conclusion is that we must have overlooked something. Maybe, in reality, the cases that demonstrate one resource constraint feeding another are conceptually different from the case that we have logically analyzed.

How can it be? Can we portray a case where one resource constraint is feeding another, and nevertheless we actually have only one resource constraint? At first sight it looks as if the question itself is absurd, but wait, maybe it does have merit. The sequential nature by which the constraints are revealed might give us a clue. The first constraint that we found was the market demand. Maybe we should restate the question by looking at the situation from the market aspect. It will now look something like this: can we portray a case where one resource constraint is feeding another, and nevertheless each market constraint is fed by only one resource constraint?

Doesn't seems to help much, but on second thought . . . Suppose that the market demand for one product places a load of one hundred percent on one resource while it places a load of only seventy percent on another resource that feeds the first one. Now suppose that the market demand for another product is placing zero load on the first resource and thirty percent on the second resource. If every time that the second resource falls behind it will give full priority to the first product, the product that created the downstream constraint, are we actually in an interactive constraint situation? You see, viewing our company through the market demanding the first product, we see the involvement of only one constraint. The other resource, even though loaded to 100%, does actually have, for our product, a lot of protective capacity. As a matter of fact, 30% of its available time, as long as we obey the priority rule above, is protective capacity for those market demands. The market demand for the second product certainly sees only one resource constraint.

Yes, we can have one resource constraint feeding another resource constraint and still be in a system without any interactive resource constraints. Our original analysis ignored the case where between the two resource constraints there is an additional outlet to the market. This type of situation not only does exist, but should be encouraged, since it leads to a much better throughput utilization of the existing investments in the resources. Of course, without obeying rigorously the above priority rule, it is a very hazardous situation—definitely for the clients of those companies.

Since we assume the existence of buffer management, we do have the mechanism to warn the work centers about significant delays—holes in the tracking and expediting zones of the origins. What we'll have to demand from the scheduling phase is, for each block having a rod pointing to a previous constraint, to print, near that block, a number. This number will simply indicate the relative importance of the fed constraint. In other words, in which iteration this resource constraint was found.

Have we finished with the scheduling phase? This, by definition, is a ridiculous question. We never finish. The number of options, like combination of resources, re-work loops, etc., is probably infinite. We have finished with the generic case that might be applicable, as is, to the vast majority of companies, but there is always more than sufficient room to do even better.

Should we now continue to develop the details of the control phase? I personally don't think so. As long as the scheduling phase is not implemented, and buffer management is done manually, any attempt to automate the local performance measurements will probably throw the company into chaos. It's better to wait and enjoy first the very significant benefits that we can gain from the implementation of the first phase of our information system, the scheduling. A concise summary of the qualitative and not just quantitative benefits is definitely in place, but we'd better leave it to the next chapter, which will serve as a summary of our discussion.

40. *Partial summary of benefits*

What are the benefits of having the scheduling phase operational in addition to the obvious benefit of being able, at last, to generate a reliable immunized schedule? Let's view it systematically from the point of view of each management function.

The first significant benefit of having the ability to have all data in memory, and thus being able to perform calculations at breath-taking speeds, is the fact that performing net requirement—finding how many units have to be produced at each point—is no longer a matter of many hours, but rather seconds. This will end the current practice of generating net requirement very infrequently and place it at the fingertips of any manager when it is needed. Net generation, as we call the attempt to calculate just the changes, will become something that belongs to the past. This awkward method, that had been developed to reduce the overwhelming computer time, has led, in many environments, to the need to constantly fight shortages. No wonder; if calculation of requirement is based on tracking changes through reported transactions, discrepancies are almost unavoidable. Speed does not only mean that we can get things faster, speed many times means the ability to get rid of very inefficient and cumbersome procedures.

But wait. If we continue in this way, this brief summary will turn into an examination of all current practices. This would, no doubt, take almost as long as all our discussion so far. Yes, we definitely have the right to be proud of overcoming so many obstacles, but we'd better restrict ourselves to a brief, concise summary of benefits.

The benefits for the material management are very clear. This system is no less than the tool that we have been waiting for for so long, the tool that MRP promised to be, but wasn't. But it seems that the benefits for production managers are almost on the same level. Everyone who has spent any time on the shop floor is too keenly aware of the constant struggle to determine the run sizes on a heavily-loaded, long set-up machine. At last we have a tool that can be really helpful in finding, not a static, but a dynamic, all-encompassing answer for the length of the runs. This new ability, combined with almost a crystal ball to predict the need for overtime, looks too good to be true. Not to mention the fact that placing a much more reliable tool in the hands of the material managers is certainly going to make the life of production personnel much simpler.

But they are not the only ones who are going to enjoy the benefits. If I am not mistaken, this is the first time that sales will be able to get a reliable pre-warning. The system will give them the ability to communicate with the production managers, not on the level of finger pointing, but on the level of common terminology—of facts and real-life considerations.

The ones who are probably going to enjoy the benefits the most are the process engineers and quality managers. Even though the dynamic buffering technique drastically reduces the lead time and inventory, its *main* benefit is actually in another area. Tracking holes in the buffer origins will, for the first time, point to the processes that must be improved, rather than to work centers that don't have enough protective capacity. Quality circles can be fed with the vitally needed information of the problems to concentrate on solving, being assured that every time a problem is solved the entire operation is going to reap benefits. This will prevent the quality circles from deteriorating to meaningless social meetings.

But probably the system, even at the stage of just the Schedule phase alone, is most important to top management. This is because, on one hand we have insisted on constructing the system in a way that it will not consider any policy constraints, and on the other hand we made sure to identify all physical constraints, and to remove all conflicts between them. The resulting schedule is immune and durable, and thus, everytime that we say "the schedule cannot be followed," the only reason for such a claim is the existence of a policy constraint. The stubbornness of not acknowledging policy constraints is exactly the thing that has turned our system into an effective tool to identify internal policy constraints.

It's quite mind-boggling to realize that all these benefits pale compared to the benefits that one can expect from the Control phase, which in turn are almost trivial compared to the main purpose of the entire system—the What-If phase. But this is definitely a subject for another discussion.

Maybe the best way to end this discussion is by reminding ourselves that we have developed this system based on the recognition of the throughput world. Today our company's culture is still too deeply immersed in the cost world. Let's not fool ourselves that it is possible to change our company's culture through a computer.

For information about other books on the
Theory of Constraints (TOC)
please visit our web site at:
www.northriverpress.com

For more information on the
Theory of Constraints (TOC)
please visit
www.goldratt.com